Dec 21 2012

TO: NANCY & THE JUDGE
HERE IS TO MORE GREAT GOLF AND
LUNCH IN THE BAR!

VERY BEST
[signature]

Reaching the Fairway

The Way It Was & The Way It Is.

By Arnold Thiesfeldt

Edited By Martin Davis

Reaching the Fairway
The Way It Was & The Way It Is.

FIRST EDITION

Published by:
The American Golfer, Inc.
200 Railroad Avenue
Greenwich, Connecticut 06830
PHONE: (203) 862-9720
FAX: (203) 862-9724
EMAIL: IMD@aol.com
WEBSITE: TheAmericanGolfer.com

ISBN: 1-888-531-18-5
EAN: 978-1-888531-183

To the many thousands of golfers who
would like the game to be more fun.

TABLE OF CONTENTS

PREFACE

BY RAY CAVE

*Former Executive Editor of Sports Illustrated, Time Magazine Managing Editor,
And Former Editorial Director of all Time, Inc. Publications*

There was golf before Tiger Woods.

There was even the business of golf before Tiger Woods.

At least that is the contention of Arnold Thiesfeldt in *Reaching the Fairway: The Way It Was & The Way It Is.*

Arnold may even be right, if you are willing to assume Arnold is the author of this book, not that other Arnold. There really was golf back then. I know, because I was there.

But what a different world it was. I was a writer for *Sports Illustrated* back in 1959. Young, but so was *SI*. Naïve, but … well, never mind. Let's just say there was a level of sports sophistication that *SI* had not yet attained. The golf editor was a devotee of track and field.

The golf writer was not the legendary Herbert Warren Wind. (And certainly not me.)

Which hardly accounts for my being assigned to write "The Sportsman of the Year" cover story on Arnold Palmer. And going to Huntington, West Virginia for a scene that explains *The Way It Was* back when you did not need to make an appointment through an agent to talk for fifteen minutes to a shortstop. And be asked, "What's in it for him?"

The Huntington Invitational was a three-day event founded, supported and dear to one Samuel Jackson Snead. Palmer, in 1960 the Masters and Open champion, had made a regular point of playing in it because Sam Snead mattered to golf, a lot, and Huntington was not all that far from Latrobe, especially when you were learning to fly your own leased jet.

So three of us are sitting on stools at the clubhouse bar following the day's play. Just Sam and Arnold and me. Them telling stories. Me shutting up. Huntington was dry then, and may still be for all I know. I haven't been back. Behind the bar was a big rack that stored say fifty liquor bottles, horizontally, with a club member's name tag under each. Arnold and I ask for Cokes or whatever. Snead leans over, squints at the names on the bottle rack and says, "I'll bet Dr. Carruthers wouldn't mind buying old Sam a drink." We'll never know if Dr. Carruthers minded or not. Or if old Sam ever paid for a drink.

It was while sitting there that Snead told Arnold if he ever wanted to have a long career and be a truly great golfer he needed to get physically fit: "Let's see how high you can kick." Arnold stood up and kicked about as high as you might or I. Snead looked dismayed, got off his stool and kicked high enough to rattle the canopy over our head. (On reflection, I'll wager he had done it many times, and won a bet each time.)

The next year I got sent to the U.S. Open to do the interviewing for a personality profile on the Hebert brothers, Lionel and Jay. Lionel was a friendly bear of a man and would invite you down to Lafayette for dirty rice. Jay was a PGA Champion and handsome as well. It had not occurred to the golf editor, or least of all me, that the U.S. Open was not the best place for interviewing in depth. I got the job done, what with Jay having a few free minutes and a gallery of five, one of which every step of the way being an attractive lady. Who? "I don't know," said Jay, "but no need to mention her. I have heard she is the good friend of a Las Vegas mobster." It was Lionel that I interviewed in depth.

That's the way it was. *SI* was young and innocent. Me too. Seen through a rear-view mirror, the times were innocent as well.

Golf was a business then too, of course, plus a way of doing serious business in a fashion long gone – to Arnold Thiesfeldt's regret, as he makes plain. Business was personal, not corporate. Face to face on the 14th green, not the 44th floor. A game for amateur golfers, not professional negotiators. A game for advertiser outings. Corporate entertaining. No game for a touring pro.

It was in 1959 that Arnold made a handshake deal with Mark McCormack, a memorable new addition to the business of agentry. McCormack had a different vision of what golfers could make from endorsements, and what corporations could reap in return. Some vision! Today Palmer still nets millions a year from businesses that use his name. (Had an Arnold Palmer ice tea lately?) But not back then. (When I was 14, I had just caddied nine holes for Byron Nelson and rushed home to tell my father I wanted to be a professional golfer. "No way, son," he said. "No money in it.")

Let's return to Huntington, West Virginia, still 1959. Arnold and I are having hamburgers in the clubhouse grill. The waitress brings them with a bottle of Hunt's ketchup. Arnold looks up at the waitress and says, "Don't you have Heinz? Well, you should." I ask Arnold, "What was that about?" He said he was paid to endorse Heinz ketchup.

Indeed he was. The winner of that year's Masters and U. S. Open was paid $10 a week – actually, nine dollars and sixty-one cents a week – to say he used Heinz ketchup. The following is from McCormack's files:

February 8, 1961. McCormack to the Heinz Company.

"We were completely shocked by the unauthorized use of Arnold Palmer's name by the H. J. Heinz Company in last week's issue of several national magazines.

"This has greatly impaired, if not completely ruined, any chance of our concluding similar arrangements with another company for a fee exceeding $5,000.

"I would greatly appreciate hearing from you or your attorneys." Blah, blah, blah.

February 16, 1961. H.J. Heinz to McCormack. "We can only conclude you do not have a copy of the enclosed contract signed by Mr. Palmer."

Oh! The enclosed contract even included advertising language in which Arnold Palmer could be quoted as saying:

"I guess I eat several hundred meals away from home every year, so naturally I've learned to size up eating places. One of the signs I go by is Heinz catsup. When I spot that familiar bottle on the table, I feel sure the food, the service and everything will be good."

That, for $9.61 a week.

All that changed dramatically in the Sixties, of course, as did *SI*'s expertise and its coverage of golf. Still especially memorable today are golf stories by Dan Jenkins, a rare writing talent then and now. (I once assigned Jenkins to cover the first college football game played on an artificial surface. As I recall his lead: "God blew it when He gave us grass.")

By mid-decade *SI* was at last making money, and the whole world of professional golf was at last doing the same. Golf had Palmer and Nicklaus and a TV audience of millions. *SI* had Dan Jenkins and a golf audience headed for millions. The world, the one we know today, was just around the corner.

So cheer it. Savor it. Wish Tiger well. But don't forget, in some quiet moment at the clubhouse bar, to reflect upon *The Way It Was.*

FOREWORD

BY DON BARR

*Former Publisher, Sports Illustrated, Executive Vice-President of Time Inc.
and Former Chairman of The First Tee of Connecticut*

I have just finished reading Ray Cave's remarks for Arnold Thiesfeldt's book, *Reaching the Fairway. The Way It Was & The Way It Is*. Ray, one of early *SI's* first golf editors, summarized the days of golf journalism beginning in the 1960s by stating that "the world, the one we know today, was just around the corner." And, throughout the succeeding decades, the game of golf has gone from relatively modest beginnings, to a country-wide expansion following World War II, as economic growth allowed more people free time and added income to allow them to enjoy the game and the lifestyle surrounding it. Today, however, the game is bumping into some realities that must be considered.

Certainly, the expense of the game is becoming a major factor in who plays and where, as is the shift in the lifestyles and schedules of those that play today. A changing family dynamic is reducing the time available for playing golf, particularly as other sports are of growing importance in young peoples' lives – and their parents' as well.

I have had the wonderful opportunity to be part of an organization that is instrumental in giving a large number of young people their first chance to become involved in golf. Thiesfeldt's first chapter mentions the decline of parents introducing their children to the game – a void filled by organizations like The First Tee.

The First Tee began in 1997 in Augusta, Georgia. Its primary mission was to develop chapters across the country, introducing golf to young people that were no longer as familiar with the sport as was the preceding generation, or who had no exposure to the game and its inherent values in the first place. The first corporate partner was the Shell Oil Company. The Masters Tournament, LPGA, PGA of America, PGA TOUR, and the USGA became the original Founding partners. The First Tee now has nearly 200 chapters nationally. In 2001, The Golf Foundation of Connecticut was founded and in 2004 the organization merged with The First Tee of Hartford to become The First Tee of Connecticut.

Golf will remain the great game as it has always been and The First Tee will continue to work hard to keep the game appealing and within reach of all those that wish to participate. Whether the game will ever return to its corporate roots as Thiesfeldt describes in his book, will probably be doubtful until the tax codes are changed in recognition of the fact that using the game as a sales tool was, and is, a legitimate business expense. An important benefit will be the job expansion this will allow in every level of the economic strata.

I do recall a day when I was the lead "salesman" on an eight-man helicopter trip to the National Golf Links of America in Southampton L.I. As the day came to a close and the Time Inc. helicopter was due to pick us up for the return to Westchester airport, I began to urge our golfers to "speed up a bit" since the chopper was due at 5:00 p.m. and there were three more holes to play. Almost instantly, several of our corporate guests pointed out that it was my helicopter for the day and "Westchester could damn well wait."

The customer was, and is, always right.

I hope you enjoy my friend Arnold's book and give careful thought to the points he makes.

The game deserves it.

INTRODUCTION

Much of this book is the result of being immersed in the advertising and publishing side of golf in the mid-1950's and 1960's at *LIFE* and *Sports Illustrated*, the 1970's at *TIME* and the early 1980's as publisher of *GOLF* Magazine. In the 1990's, I became involved with two new start-up publications, *LINKS* Magazine and *Senior Golfer*.

To that list, one should add wandering the fairways of Kittanning Country Club in the mid-1940's, a beautiful nine-hole course in Western Pennsylvania where I was introduced to the game. Next, would be six years in the early 1960's at Tedesco County Club in Marblehead, Massachusetts, where I met some of the most memorable characters the game had to offer. Then, a few short years at Oakland Hills Country Club in Michigan in the 1970's, and finally, a 40-plus year stay at Winged Foot Golf Club in Mamaroneck, New York. Lastly, add two years at Seaview Golf Club in Atlantic City where customer golf was the order of the day.

I couldn't possibly list all the public or resort courses that ought to go on the roster, except to say that at least one hundred courses and resorts in and out of the United States have witnessed my hook. Included on the list are some of the finest courses in the Bay Area, Los Angeles, Michigan, New York, New England, Ireland, Scotland, Spain and Italy.

Some have said that what is written on the pages that follow is a book about the advertising business as much as it is about golf. It is true that what is recorded here deals with how golf became entwined with various corporate and marketing personnel all the way from the early 1950's and 60's through the 90's and now this entry in 2012.

But, the book is also a record about the way golf, and particularly business golf, actually is today. A normal initiation fee in a private club can run upwards of $150,000 with annual dues of $10 – $12,000 or more at a large metropolitan club. Daily fees in certain well-known public facilities can be in the $150 to $300 range. Given the recent recession, some of those fees are dropping, but the dues and assessments seem to continually rise.

Today, no company will put up exorbitant amounts of money for an employee's golf initiation fee. What was known as "relationship marketing," a descriptor for developing a close, personal relationship with a customer has been seriously and perhaps permanently impaired. Travel to and from major golf destinations by corporate jet had to be discontinued, and regular involvement in weekend golf matches is increasingly falling victim to newer members that play early in the morning and, surprisingly, often by themselves.

The original concept for business-related golfing trips typically consisted of three foursomes of key ad agency personnel or executives from a client company plus a fourth foursome of host personnel. They would leave early Thursday morning, arriving at their destination at noon. Friday and Saturday would be devoted to attending an event or playing golf or both. The evenings were devoted to dinner conversation, a few drinks, and cards. They would arrive back home Saturday evening a very happy group of campers, indeed!

The question has been asked if we can get those old trips back, many of which are detailed in this account. I'm afraid that they may be gone forever just as we are losing diversity within the membership rosters of the clubs we join. Increasingly, many school teachers, local lawyers and businessmen, clergy, and surprisingly, even many doctors are being left behind financially and it is hurting the ultimate judgements made by and for a given club. Rick Pitino, the famed college basketball coach said it best in the 1996 U.S. Open issue of *Links* Magazine about his Winged Foot membership: "On any given day, you can play with a chairman of one our largest companies and the next day play with a school teacher." Unfortunately, we are also losing many of the great characters of the game as various categories of members are squeezed financially.

Claude Harmon, the famous teaching professional from Winged Foot, Seminole and Thunderbird in Palm Springs is no longer telling golf stories at Mike Manuche's on West 52nd St. as he did on many an evening during the early '60s. Dick Maylander, a wonderful salesman from *LIFE* and *TIME* is no longer hosting Penny Tweedy of Secretariat fame as he did at his annual Christmas party for Phillip Morris executives in the early '70s. And Jack Mandable, long-time Advertising Director for *Newsweek*, and Bob Young, retired Ad Director at *The New Yorker* are probably still annoyed at

TIME's golf trips on the F27 to the Masters in the '70s and '80s. You should get an F27 if you are going to compete with *TIME!*

Finally, this book deals with the show business aspect of today's tournament golf on television. Some feel that TV tournament coverage has become a sport all by itself. Others say that the current focus of our media has created a golfing public so cynical that if a top player falters, he or she is instantly relegated to the junk heap. It is an attitude that not only demeans top amateur levels of golf, but an attitude that, on occasion, carries over to other forms of excellence in American endeavors.

STATE OF THE GAME

CHAPTER I

PRESIDIO. SAN FRANCISCO, CALIFORNIA. JUNE 1955

In the early '50s, LIFE Magazine, still a premiere national publication in those years, took advantage of a rapidly growing public interest in golf by creating a nationwide golf event involving the many thousands of LIFE readers with golf handicaps. The idea was that golfers across the country could turn in a score from their own clubs to be matched against the scores of that year's four national champions. National Golf Day had a date that was designated to be just prior to the 1955 U.S. Open to be held at The Olympic Club in San Francisco.

In 1955, Ed Furgol was the defending U.S. Open champion, Patty Berg was the Women's Open champion and Gene Andrews was the Publinx champ. There was a substitute for the defending U.S. Junior champion. Since I was working on my very first job for LIFE in San Francisco as a Retail Representative in the Advertising Department, I was invited to fill out one of the National Golf Day foursomes to be played at the Army base golf course at the Presidio.

On the day of play, a young man probably 17 or 18 years old started to walk toward me. I told him that "mine was the red bag on the rack." He had blond hair with a cowlick, a white tee shirt and khaki pants, and was slightly pigeon-toed. An army sergeant from the base suddenly stepped in and said that, "the young man was not a caddy, but he would be playing with me that day." The sergeant's name tag said Geiberger.

The sergeant's younger brother, Al, was subbing for that year's U.S. Junior champ and was going to attend the University of Southern California the next year. That day, I think he played a reasonably tough Presidio course in 73 strokes. I always wanted to tell Al when I saw him years later in a competition, particularly at the Masters, that, "when he got through with his round, he could pick up the red bag for a late afternoon loop!" I never got that chance. Al went on to win 11 times on the PGA TOUR (including the 1966 PGA Championship), 10 times on the Champions Tour, was on the 1967 and '75 Ryder Cup teams and was the first to shoot an official 59 on the TOUR.

〜〜〜〜〜〜〜

When I first started to write down all the wonderful things that have happened to the game over the years, I began to realize that so much is changing in golf and its venues that while a great deal has gone right, even more has strayed off course.

Question one might be: "What will be the future of a game that now requires many thousands of dollars just to join a club?" A sport that once boasted of bringing an "every man" approach to its membership is now becoming the province of the very rich. And instead of humility, today's country club membership is headed towards the almost unwitting attitudes that enormous member incomes generate. Some say that if you don't run a hedge fund, you've got little chance of joining a well-known club.

And even if you do get through the doors, reaching today's fairways, never mind hitting them, now requires a cannon. As more and more golf courses are set up by ex-professional players for professional style play, the game is no longer played on a pleasant piece of grass. I belong to a club that has put in a 650-yard par 5 for tournament play, and there is concern on the part of a few, that it may not be long enough. There has even been some talk in golf circles of an 8,000 yard course being the norm in the future. I think I'm getting old just in time.

Complicating the obvious physical problems of today's golf courses, i.e. overall length, weed control, dwindling water supplies and bunkering further down our fairways, the sport is now making more and more appearances in the courtroom. Not only is Martha Burk worried about breaking into a legally-established club that has only male members (Augusta National Golf Club), there are now even more legal questions about a private club's right to pick members purely on a like or dislike basis. Candidates that are turned down are not only threatening to sue, but have actually done so. More mundane issues such as when spouses can or cannot play or who can go in what grillroom – and when, have often moved quickly towards courtrooms.

Finally, we may be watching the early signs of suburban politicians being forced to answer questions about the last vestiges of "available space" for their communities. One attractive consideration could be the legal sale of large tracts of land that for years have been the property of private clubs. "Eminent domain" has already made an appearance in at least one state supreme court. At the very least, there is a danger of taking away a golf club's current favorable tax status.

And while we're talking about taking away property, the great sports-oriented watering holes like Manuche's, Toots Shor's and Rose's in mid-town Manhattan, are now gone and with their closing, some of the closest ties between businessmen, spectators and well-known athletes have passed into history as well. Today, the closest you are going to get to a famous athlete is through his agent and even then, it is doubtful that you'll meet the star unless guaranteed millions are on the table. Still, there are some recent signs that humility, courtesy of the Darren Clarkes' of the world, may be making occasional, but welcome, appearances in the game.

In a very real sense, golf clubs in the 60's and 70's were a weekend extension of the restaurant scene. Media customers in those early years were allowed by their companies, even encouraged, to be invited to wonderful venues of golf, e.g., Pinehurst, Augusta during the Masters, National Golf Links on Long Island, Pine Valley and Seaview in New Jersey, Seminole in Florida and Harbour Town in Hilton Head. Even the IRS allowed corporations to deduct these items as sales expenses, which, in those days were exactly that! Many long-lasting relationships were built and many of those were very funny and most were uniquely memorable.

It is doubtful if the golfing world will see another Steve Clow, who oversaw the American Airlines account at Doyle Dane

Bernbach. There was a day when Steve put the entire Time Inc. Fairchild's $2,500 fuel bill on his credit card to show his appreciation at being invited on a Sea Island trip. The pilots straightened out the situation, but no one who was there will ever forget a man named Steve Clow!

Or Hank Malfa, then president of Cunningham and Walsh on a *TIME* Magazine golf trip to Florida. He was overheard in an early morning phone conversation with his wife, who was stuck back in New York, in the middle of one of the worst blizzards of the winter. At the time of the phone call, it was 80 degrees in Florida under brilliant skies.

In reply to her question about the weather he was experiencing on his trip, Hank replied sympathetically, "that it had just stopped snowing in Florida." Hank correctly figured that would hold the peace until at least lunch hour.

Alas, it has all changed. Corporations now forbid its employees to get involved with any form of entertainment that could be construed as a bribe. The old "hang outs" in the various midtowns across the country could no longer keep their doors open. Coincidental with this change, the very golf clubs that were involved in much of this entertainment were undergoing their own monumental changes.

In the place of funding club memberships, many corporations are now investing thousands of dollars in huge bouts of entertainment, including the hospitality tents that now line professional championship courses. The "new approved" method of getting to know a customer is to put them in a roomful of other customers where no one knows the other, nor is it likely that they will ever get to know one another.

The National Golf Foundation, the organization that keeps track of the number of people that participate in golf, has recently provided playing totals that are a stark reminder of how fragile the economics of today's game may be.

The NGF, at one point in their reporting, defined a "core" golfer as a person, age 18 or older, who played at least eight times a year. In the latest NGF study, their core golfer is now six-years-old and up, but still playing eight-plus rounds annually. I am not sure how many rounds six-year-olds are playing these days, but the total of core golfers is dropping. In 2005, the total was 18.0 million people in the category while the total in 2010 was down to 14.8 million.

Another key category in the NGF study is "avid" golfers, i.e. those who play 25-plus rounds a year. In 2005, avid golfers totaled 9.1 million. Just five years later, that total was down to seven million golfers. Since most of the golf equipment is sold to this group and they make up the bulk of all golf rounds played, any drop in this group is crucial to golf's health.

And here's another set of numbers that should nail it all down. The NGF says that currently there are 4,262 private clubs in the U.S. They also have on record 9,233 daily fee courses and 2,395 municipal courses. Further, public golfers are responsible for 75% of the rounds played and dollars spent on golf.

A friend of mine from the early days of *Sports Illustrated*, the late

Dick Haskell, who subsequently served as the Executive Director of the Massachusetts Golf Association, watched the game's culture change dramatically over his 29 years in that position. Haskell felt that the decline in the number of rounds played in the U.S. over the past few years may be permanent. He cited the steep rise in caddie fees, ever-higher greens fees and, most particularly, sky-high initiation charges. All of this, in combination with the shift toward non-golf family activities, is a major hindrance to golf's growth.

You can also get a good idea of where the game is headed from another NGF survey number that indicates that 60% of the new courses being built in the U.S. will be real estate-oriented. That is in line with all course development in the U.S. over the past 20 years. It also reflects the number of Americans who want a golf course right next to their retirement home with a financial package that makes it easy to move away from their New York or Chicago or Boston or Seattle "hometown."

Add to all this, the current crush of a recession has now forced new properties to charge a set fee to all homeowners surrounding the development's golf course rather than letting members by themselves handle club expenses. Less productive golf seasons and area home values are better protected by widening the financing of the adjacent club.

Haskell also proposed one of the most penetrating questions I have ever heard about today's game: Is the game itself really as much fun as we usually hope for? He suggested that the imagined amount of enjoyment simply doesn't exist when most people are almost invariably disappointed with their score.

To that point, one could ask if we should keep score at all? Why we can't play seven holes or 11 holes once in a while? Why 18, indeed? Certainly nine holes can get the job done in most casual rounds. In far too many clubs, caddie fees are rising so that, increasingly, nine holes become almost mandatory. Jack Nicklaus is now lobbying for a 12-hole course and Barney Adams, the well-known golf-equipment manufacturer, is suggesting moving the tees forward instead of constantly back. According to some recent reports, even the United States Golf Association and the PGA of America seem to be reacting positively to their ideas. I do hear the word "fun" more and more as golfers move up to where an iron will once again reach a green.

Many more in the game now suggest that average golfers are now paying little or no attention to the original concept of the game: refreshment of the soul, camaraderie, and the appreciation of the setting itself. Keeping tabs on our own ability through a recorded score may, indeed, be getting in the way of benefiting from the essential beauty of the game. After all, when we took up games as a child, we played whatever was in front of us for the fun of it. We played softball, or tennis, or touch football without comparing our individual abilities to achieve a ranking unless we were planning to turn professional.

I recently posed the Haskell question of how much "fun" people may or may not be having, to a group of golfing friends and their answer was surprising. They all agreed that their games were not very satisfactory but they also asked, "What would be the alternative to playing golf?"

I hadn't expected that their answer would be that "golf simply fills up four to five hours in their lives and gets them out of the house." If that is the case, one ought to have a thousand ways for building a very enjoyable day doing things that have absolutely nothing to do with playing golf.

Otherwise, you might just as well get a job that you don't like.

Here's a contemporary father talking about today's game:

"I would love to spend more time at the golf course with my kids, but it just doesn't work out the way it did when I started golf with my dad. Anyway, we've got a soccer game at 2:30, a swim meet at 4:00, and basketball practice at 7:30."

If you were a young man in the 1940's and 1950's, going to the golf club meant engaging with adults and spending an entire afternoon playing golf. You paid attention to what Mr. Moore said about drinking and driving. You learned from Mr. Miller what it took to run a Ford dealership. You came out of it with a deep understanding of the game, an appreciation of what the adult world expected from young people and most important, three-and-a -half special hours with your dad. And in the summer, during the week, when you weren't playing, you caddied for 50 cents a bag.

While there is less golf with Mr. Moore and Mr. Miller these days, on a very positive note there is now evidence that several organizations are starting to fill that void. One, in particular, that comes to mind is The First Tee of Connecticut, part of an extensive nationwide organization. The chairman of that organization was Don Barr, a former publisher of *Sports Illustrated* and an Executive Vice President of Time Inc.

According to Barr, recently retired from The First Tee organization, and current president David Polk, some 50,000 youngsters were introduced to the game and its traditions in Connecticut through 2011. Nationally, the organization has introduced the game to 4.7 million young participants since 1997, and has established their National School Program in more than 4,000 elementary schools across the country. Incidentally, the chief executive of the national organization is Joe Louis Barrow, Jr., the son of heavyweight boxing champion, Joe Louis.

Tradition is being further rattled by a changing dress code. Ties are gone at cocktail parties. Don't bother with a jacket. Wear blue jeans to the office. When Winged Foot finally went along with the current thinking that men could wear shorts on the course in the summer, I got a call from my oldest son, at the time, age 35, who expressed disappointment with the new rule. I asked him why he was so concerned and he replied that the original dress code at Winged Foot was "special."

He went on to explain, "When I was growing up, I had to wear a jacket and tie to go to a Sunday luncheon at the club with the family and I had to wear long pants on the course."

"It was something special that I'll never forget," he added.

Traditions are disappearing from competition itself. Too many club and amateur events including member-guests are often deadly serious and not very polite.

"Are you going to the cocktail party tonight?" one player might casually ask.

"You had a six on the last hole, not a five," might be the reply. All in all, not very conducive to a friendly round.

Egos are exposed. Arguments simmer. People who are close friends and associates in the clubhouse are changing their stripes in official club competitions. A great number of people have given up on intra-club tournaments altogether. And, if you do play in one of these events, bring money. Most of these member-guests often go on somebody's expense account, but if you have to pay for it yourself, plan for at least $1,000 or more for three guests during the entire day.

Golf is now being intersected by a perfect storm of high prices and costs, all mixed into a major shift in family cultures and traditions. Whatever happens I, for one, feel that the game is heading toward major changes, which will demand some major an-swers – and profound soul-searching.

BACK TO THE BEGINNING

CHAPTER 2

NEW YORK CITY, AUGUST, 1958

No accounting of the giant steps golf has taken over the past 50 years would be complete without including the early years of Sports Illustrated. *It started in August of 1954. The nation was just getting into the high gear of a massive new economy created after World War II. Henry Luce, the founder of Time Inc., always tried to have one word titles for his properties, i.e., TIME, LIFE, Fortune, and Sport. The only problem was there was already a magazine called Sport and they were not about to give up the title. It took a while for people to get used to the word, "Illustrated." Anyone looking at the world of golf today, would be hard-pressed to understand that the magazine's sales representatives, probably 40 strong, had to go into America's industrial heartland and, literally plead with the management of those companies that, "All sports, including golf, could help sell their products!" SI had offices in probably 10 major cities around the country and in looking back, it is hard to imagine that those early pioneers could pull it all off.*

~~~~~~~~~~

Here we are five decades later paying someone named Alex Rodriguez $250 million to hit a split-seam fastball, and all he has to do is hit it one out of three tries. And, the Tiger Woods' of the world could win only a measly $500,000 just by finishing third.

When the magazine premiered, the nation was still very much guided by a strong Protestant work ethic allowing very few to play golf during the workweek. A current issue of *LINKS* Magazine refers to a time "when golf came to the U.S with an old world instruction kit for how to play it ethically and even how to use the game to build character."

To help introduce *Sports Illustrated,* the new management of the magazine leased out an assortment of very famous downtown locations across the country, i.e., the skating rink at Rockefeller Center, State Street in Chicago, Union Square in San Francisco and the Golden Triangle in Pittsburgh, et al. The plan called for well-known athletes to put on exhibitions in sports such as football, basketball, badminton, golf, tennis and swimming. They were put to work at noon or at day's end to let people see first-hand how the world of sport could excite and move a crowd.

Ann Marston, an Olympic archery champion, shot "bulls-eyes" on targets in Rockefeller Center. In San Francisco's Union Square, Quarterback Frankie Albert of the 49ers threw passes to star receiver Gordie Soltau, the ex-Minnesota great. Bobby Riggs and Ken Rosewall put on tennis exhibitions in several major city centers.

Claude Harmon, 1948 Masters Champion from nearby Winged Foot, gave golfing demonstrations along with Harry Obitz and Dick Farley in their "The Swing's the Thing" Golf School, again in Rockefeller Center with the ice removed. In 1964, Harmon was featured on the cover of the magazine with a series of golf lessons for an increasingly interested American public. Another featured athlete was Donna de Varona who had just come back as a successful teenage swimmer from the Olympics and just a few years ago, returned from Shanghai where the fate of New York City as an Olympic site was being determined.

Simultaneously, *Sports Illustrated* invented what was called the "Living Room Show." A "typical" subscriber's living room was set up in various hotels and auditoriums across the country. The nation's advertisers were invited for a luncheon showing. The subscriber's living room included pictures, paintings, and the reasonably expensive furniture that a *Sports Illustrated* reader would likely have in his or her home. In one corner was a bar with all the leading liquors of the day. In another corner was a library complete with trophies and mementos from the reader's various trips. Advertising guests were encouraged to use the quite comfortable living room couches and chairs while the new magazine's mandate was explained to the marketing industry.

Each wall opened to a different part of the *SI* story. One wall opened to statistics that described the readership of the magazine. The next was a celebrity athlete that talked about the value of sports to both individuals and the business community. The final wall was an editor who talked about the direction the coverage of the magazine was taking.

The athletes/presenters at the time were all well known and in need of second off-season jobs. Kyle Rote, with his quiet Texas accent was an instant hit as was Pat Summerall who really began his announcing career doing emcee work for several *SI* shows and presentations while he was still a New York Giant.

No one recognized it at the time but the "Living Room Show", as it was known on Madison Avenue, was the first major "life style" presentation the advertising business had ever seen. As much as anything, this early and unique presentation moved the magazine into a highly visible position in the advertising community.

One of my own early assignments on the *Sports Illustrated* sales staff was to get out to the Philadelphia airport and pick up the very famous Sam Snead. I was to bring him to lunch in Camden, N.J. with a group of executives from the Campbell Soup Company. Snead and Ben Hogan were still contesting one another in those days, and I was not only duly impressed, I was as nervous as I've ever been anywhere.

Since I had never met Mr. Snead, I had no idea of what to expect. Keith Morris, who was *SI's* Special Promotions Director, told me Sam was very kind and affable. Keith obviously didn't include that day's Sam Snead. Sam was in a hurry, impatient and not very talkative on the drive to Camden. A group of perhaps twenty Campbell Soup executives were waiting for us in the company dining room.

The executives were delighted to have this chance to talk to a legend. Things ran smoothly until coffee was served. One of the Campbell Soup people said that he had heard that Sam liked their tomato juice in the large cans.

Sam acknowledged that he did, indeed, and asked, "Would they ship him a couple of cases of the tomato juice?"

"And make sure it's the large cans." added Snead.

"Absolutely", replied one of the executives who also asked, "Do you really like our tomato juice that much?"

"Oh, hell no, I throw the damned juice out," Sam said. "I just bury my money in the cans!"

I thought I was watching my short career get shorter. Fortunately, it was a golf lunch and all 20 executives broke up in laughter. We were both asked to come back.

Mentioning the name Keith Morris, brings up a name that few people in sports ever talk about today. Keith was extraordinarily important in mixing athletes into the marketing of products. A large part of the early *Sports Illustrated* merchandising activity was originated by a brilliant promotion man named George Trescher, who put Keith in charge of what eventually became famous as the "Speaker's Bureau." He and Trescher were among the first to recognize that top-name athletes, and professional golfers soon thereafter, could point the way to the future of merchandise "branding." Incidentally, Trescher helped Arnold Scassi, the well-known fashion designer, in his career's beginning by reversing his real last name, Issacs.

There were, of course, some important business agents already operating in the world of sports like Fred Corcoran who promoted Sam Snead, Babe Zaharias, Ted Williams and Stan Musial. But it was Keith that built the first complete stable of well-known athletes to be used by advertisers for various promotions, advertisements, or at dinner engagements.

Had Keith decided to take the concept out on his own, there might not have been the International Management Group that we know today or its founder, Mark McCormack. McCormack became, almost instantly, the leading sports promoter in the country by signing Arnold Palmer, Jack Nicklaus, and Gary Player. Keith, however, decided that he liked the magazine world much better than running his own company.

But, as the world would quickly note, McCormack was very much aware of what Morris and *SI* were building. When Arnold won the 1954 U.S. Amateur in Cleveland, McCormack signed him a few years later and began to expand his own group of athletes, involving them also with the merchandising of various products. McCormack, of course, went on to head IMG for many years and became one of the most powerful figures in the world of sport.

Looking back, there wasn't anybody, including Luce that had an idea it would all become as big as it eventually did. It was also very true that without Luce's vision, *Sports Illustrated* might not have had its enormous staying power in those early days. Today's publishers might have killed it off when it went for a number of years before turning its first profit.

What has been of little note in the history of *SI* was that a meeting that occurred between *Sports Illustrated* and CBS executives in the late 1950s.

The network decided to televise a limited number of sports events on the weekends, and *SI* responded by moving its closing date from Friday night to Sunday night in order to write about what had gone on the air over the weekend. It was a critical and successful decision that was to take *SI* from the rather esoteric world of polo and shooting, horses and dog shows, to the hardcore world of football, basketball, track, hockey and boxing. Boxing, of course, had its Gillette Friday Night Fights on TV, but the weekends presented the most promising activities for a nation that was simultaneously beginning to switch its lifestyle activities to center around the living room television. Golf was included in the *SI* editorial format when no one had a clue as to how important the game, particularly the professional game, would eventually become.

I should have known how popular the magazine would eventually be by the reaction of one of my first advertising sales customers. *SI* had developed a New York Metropolitan Edition that was designed to show local customers and particularly, ad agencies, how appropriate the magazine would be as an advertising vehicle. Jim Hayes, who went on to be the Publisher of *Fortune* and I were on that very first sales staff for that edition. Mary Phelan, a very bright merchandising specialist was the first female member of the sales staff, worked on that edition, and a wonderful salesman named Mac Johnson was our boss.

The early customer I refer to was a men's clothing retailer named Edward Reed Ltd. on 49th St. just across from the old Time-Life Building near the skating rink. Johnson sent me over to Edward Reed following a brief morning sales meeting.

I was back in the Time-Life Building in about 20 minutes with an order for 12 columns of advertising to run on a once-a-month basis. Johnson was suitably impressed with the speed of the transaction and said so.

What Johnson did not know, nor did I tell him, is that I had purchased a suit from the store just the day before. Still, without the increasing popularity of the publication, no sale would have happened at that speed.

The owner also invited me out to his golf course later that summer.

A major part of those early days was Ray Cave, one of the first golf editors for the magazine. Ray went on to be Executive Editor of *Sports Illustrated* but at a sales meeting in Florida, he introduced a new writer from Texas by the name of Dan Jenkins. In the early 1960s, few people in New York had ever heard of Dan and had no idea what to expect. All Ray said was that Dan would revolutionize golf writing. Indeed he did, with a fresh style of sports writing that would shake the reverential reporting styles of Herbert Warren Wind and the other headliners of the day. Dan went on to write the memorable *Dogged Victims of Inexorable Fate* and wrote the book that produced the hit movie, *Semi-Tough*.

Ray eventually became *TIME's* Managing Editor and ultimately, the company's Editorial Director for all publications, but in the meantime, Dan almost instantly captured the attention of millions. One of his most powerful pieces was called "The Glory Game," a chapter in *Dogged Victims.* The chapter was the story about Dan's early playing days at a public course next to his alma mater, Texas

Christian University. Dan referred to the course as "Goat Hills." Its real name was Worth Hills and it was in Fort Worth. Damon Runyon could not have dreamed up more colorful characters to be one's golf associates. Weldon the Oath, Moron Tom, and Cecil the Parachute were three of Dan's favorites. Cecil the Parachute got his name by lurching off the ground and falling down as he hit his drives.

A fascinated golfing nation copied the characters in Jenkin's book "who played from the first tee at Goat Hills to the third green at Colonial Country Club roughly fifteen blocks away." Another hole they invented was known as the Thousand Yard Dash which started at the Goat Hills' 12th green and ended in a hole on the concrete clubhouse porch. Dan eighteen putted for a 23, while Foot the Free one-putted for a six, the best hole Dan says he ever saw played. You could also play in a foursome from a local bar known as Lake Austin, "to a brown loafer in the closet of a University of Texas apartment" wrote Dan in *The Glory Game*.

Interestingly, in a TV news show that called attention to the 50th anniversary of the magazine, Dan said that he had stopped writing for *SI* because "it had changed its direction in writing requirements." It is true that today's magazines, including *Sports Illustrated* are using much shorter stories than ever before. But it is also true, however, that much literary effort today is shaped by the internet with its almost casual style.

At about the same time that Ray and Dan were beginning to record the progress of professional golf, CBS had already made a decision to televise a relatively-unknown invitational golf event in Augusta, Georgia named the Masters Tournament. No decision was better for the world of golf, or for that matter for the entire world of sport. And no one captured those early days better than Dan.

Several years ago, I had the pleasure of having lunch with Ray Cave in Manhattan. Despite our discussion of the early *SI* years, Ray was quick to point out that there would have been no *Sports Illustrated* had there been no televised sports."

Indeed, here came Arnie charging out of the Georgia pines, hitching his trousers and chain-smoking cigarettes, straight into the nation's living rooms. Some say that if Jack had come along before Arnold, golf's wild popularity would have been put off until another Arnie came along. What was remarkable about Arnold was his unfailing ability, even in the middle of intense competition, to make spectators and fans feel welcome and comfortable in his presence.

He won his first Masters in 1958. In 1960, Arnold won both the Masters and the U.S. Open. He was on *SI's* cover as "Sportsman of the Year" in 1960.

A footnote to Arnie's first win at Augusta in 1958 is that the total number of people who now claim to have been there for that event, greatly exceeds the number of people that were in attendance at the last dozen Super Bowls!

Later in the fall of 1958, NBC televised the National Football League's championship game between the New York Giants and the

Baltimore Colts. The first professional football championship game to be televised nationally was in 1951, but the game in 1958 had so many stars, including Charley Conerly, Johnny Unitas, Frank Gifford and Kyle Rote that the press – along with the entire country – became fascinated by the outcome.

In fact, in 2008, Gifford wrote a commemorative book about that event, which, like the chapter in Jenkins' book, was also called "The Glory Game." Gifford wrote that the overtime that ended the game had 45 million people and 11 million households watching as Alan Ameche crossed the goal line for the Colts win. And that was fifty-four years ago!

Coming after Palmer's appearance on TV in the spring of the year, the success of that televised championship game forever changed the worth of the individual stars in every imaginable sport including NASCAR.

The entire world of sport, based in large degree on the Masters and Palmer and the championship game, took on a dimension that would eventually lead American industry to bid on huge financial contracts for various sports events. Along with the use of sport to help brand merchandise, the athletes themselves were also starting to sign large contracts to represent those same companies in all forms of promotion and endorsement. Until the revelation that athletes could also generate tremendous interest in a line of products, the leading golf money winner in 1958 earned $45,000 in prize money!

As the scribes often put it, "The rest is history." Arnie showed the nation's marketers what star power could do in conjunction with television. I'll bet a lunch with Martha Burk that she wasn't watching CBS during Palmer's momentous weeks at Augusta National! And I'll also bet that most of today's young millionaire athletes, in sport after sport, have no idea how much they personally owe to Arnold. Or even to Keith Morris or Dan Jenkins or Ray Cave.

CORPORATE CLIENTS

CHAPTER 3

AUGUSTA, GEORGIA. 1961

In the mid-1960s, Daniel Field, an airport outside of Augusta, Georgia, was popular for private aircraft bringing people to the Masters. On the main entrance, one of the doors had a sign that said "No Spikes Please." That should give you an idea of how many private planes were coming in and out of the airport on tournament days. Even The New York Times *spotted the extraordinary number and ran a picture in the paper of the aircraft parked in rows. It caused such a ruckus, that many of the corporations began to fly their planes into other nearby airfields so that they would not be so noticeable.*

~~~~~~~~~~~~~~~~~~~~~~~

Arthur Keylor, an Executive Vice-President of Time Inc., when that kind of a title carried some weight, once offered the *TIME* sales staff a chance to get their advertising guests to destinations like the Masters or a noted golf resort more quickly by using a corporate G2 jet. The usual plane used for such trips was an older, albeit, much slower Fairchild F27 with the overhead engines. The Fairchild would get to Florida in a little over four hours. The G2 took 1½ hours to cover the same distance.

"Why don't you use the G2?" asked Keylor.

"OK, great," said the New York Sales Manager.

Keylor wanted to know how the trip went when everybody got back in the office.

"I think we may have to go back to the Fairchild", said the Sales Manager.

"Why?" a disappointed Keylor asked.

"Well, to be honest Art, the G2 doesn't take long enough" offered the manager.

The whole idea in those days was to get customers as far away from daily responsibilities as one could. And a major part of the fun was to have breakfast on board the F27 at 7:30 AM and play gin rummy for a few hours before landing in Florida or some other amenable destination. In fact, one guest annually arrived at Hangar "G" at Westchester airport for the Masters trip with enough Mimosas for the entire group.

No one ever heard about the G2 ever again.

The idea of "getting away" was probably best personified by a Cleveland ad agency executive who went to the Masters every year but had never played a round of golf in his life. In the 1960's, *Sports Illustrated* rented what was, literally, the Old Government House for the city of Augusta. The large ramshackle old building became a town landmark but was opened for special occasions like housing guests for Masters week.

The Cleveland guest arose each morning of his stay later than the other guests since he wasn't a golfer. Following a leisurely brunch he repaired to a large enameled bathtub filled with steaming hot water. It even had lion's paw legs. He took with him a very large-stem martini and sank deep in the hot water up to his neck, taking an occasional sip from his drink that was positioned on the wooden sideboard. Two enormously helpful housekeepers with the names, "Evening Cal" and "Morning Cal", were given the task of checking on him occasionally. They obviously got their names from the shift that they worked.

"You OK?" they would call through the bathroom door.

"Couldn't be better," came the reply. Thankfully, neither Cal ever got total silence in return.

It was debated for years as to who had the better time, those watching the Masters or the man from Cleveland with his daily hot tub and his martini.

"Morning Cal" and "Evening Cal" had one additional but unforeseen assignment. Early each morning, some 16 *Sports Illustrated* guests at the Old Government House, not used to sleeping quarters so unfamiliar, finally gave up on sleeping and got up to play at least a half-dozen gin games. Later in the day, the lack of sleep would eventually catch up with all 16, but the gin games sure took care of how to spend sleepless early morning hours while waiting for breakfast!

On one occasion, a guest jumped out of the F27. Fortunately, the airplane was already on the ground when he jumped. He had apparently decided that he would like to get something out of his golf bag, which he spotted being loaded onto the aircraft. Before anyone could say anything, he dropped the 15 feet to the ground and broke his ankle. Asked why he jumped he said, "I thought it was only a few feet." Nevertheless, he threatened to sue for his injury and the issue was settled out of court. A good customer has certain advantages.

At dinner one evening, a number of *SI's* Augusta golfing visitors were openly debating who was the toughest boxer that any one of them had ever seen. The argument ranged around the table.

"Rocky Graziano," said one.

"Jake LaMotta was the toughest fighter I ever saw," said another.

"Harry Wadkins," interjected one of the guests.

"Who in the world is Harry Wadkins?" the entire table wanted to know since no one had ever heard the name.

"Harry Wadkins beat the hell out of me when I was 11-years old." The guest was Carl Ally, one of the top ad agency executives in New York.

Not all trips went that smoothly. John deGarmo, chairman of his own very successful ad agency in New York had just made an offer to Chet Posey of McCann Erickson to be deGarmo's new President and CEO. Posey accepted and was to start on the following Monday. One of his new assignments was to handle financial matters. First, however, they would be paired over the weekend in the annual Devereux Milburn golf tournament played at Palmetto Golf Club in Aiken, South Carolina, just outside of Augusta, and hosted by the old French Amateur champion, Bobby Knowles.

The well-attended event was played just before Masters week. On opening day, Saturday, the pair found themselves in first place at 13-under par when 16-under would usually win the two-day championship plus a large chunk of a very sizeable Calcutta. Since they didn't go to the Calcutta on Saturday night, the usual custom was to offer buying half of their team from the successful bidder, but only before they teed off for the second round.

John and Chet teed off first on Day Two.

"Chet, how much did our team go for?" asked John as they were walking off the first tee.

"I don't know. I thought you were going to look into it," Posey said.

I turned to my partner, Bruce Durkee, an old friend from Tedesco Country Club outside Boston, who had played in two U.S Amateurs and one Senior Amateur, and said "Let's get the hell out of here." Several thousand dollars had potentially just gone down the drain.

We walked down the opposite side of the fairway trying to stay out of the way of Madison Avenue's latest "hot" executive team. They went on to be a very successful business combination.

But, I'm not sure if they ever played in a golf tournament together again.

Speaking of golf tournaments, some stories have to be recorded whether they are true or not. Lenny Clark, another long-time player at Tedesco, was invited to play in a member-guest in Rhode Island. He accepted with trepidation, because his partner's victory the year before had them teeing off first. Lenny was a delightful member of the club but a less-than-average golfer. Since he was about to tee off in front of some 200 people, he asked a friend what he should do under the circumstances.

The friend counseled that he "should have a positive thought in mind and hit the ball as hard as he could."

Len took his stance with the positive thought in mind and swung. The ball skipped across a small pond in front of the tee, ricocheted off the bank on the far side, and back into the clubhouse clock. The glass on the face of the clock exploded across the patio with everybody diving for cover.

It was reported later, that Lenny's ball came to rest within four feet of the spot from where Lenny had hit it. Lenny's summary of the situation was that the tournament had cost him $100 for a new face on the clock before he had been on the course less than half a minute!

In those days, not all corporate golf guests had to be entertained or even be entertaining like Lenny. Some of them were invited to be speakers at sales meetings for various magazine staffs. At one *Sports Illustrated* gathering at Dorado Beach in Puerto Rico, attendees were quite surprised to learn that there would be no speaker on the last night of the conference. Also unusual was the location for the dinner. It was in a hall big enough for at least four dinner groups each of them our size.

Dinner progressed toward dessert when a door opened at the far end of the outer hall. A single figure came out of the gloom toward the dinner tables with what appeared to be a rifle slung over his shoulder. As the man grew closer we could see that the "rifle" was a golf club. We could also see that the man had the slightly splay-footed walk of a Bob Hope – because he was Bob Hope!

The surprise was on us. Hope had been officially invited to be the dinner speaker. As Hope moved toward the lectern, the group broke into Hope's theme song, "Thanks for the Memories." Hope went on to provide laugh after laugh for well over an hour. He related his days on the stage as well as his matches on and off the golf course. No dinner speaker was ever more welcome or more beloved.

Hope's connection with golf is, of course, legendary. Toward the later years in Gene Sarazen's life, Gene was being interviewed on Golf Channel and was asked about his own most vivid golf memories. He instantly related a moment from his days as a young assistant professional at Pelham Country Club in Pelham, New York. Sarazen's on-air story, as closely as I can recall it, involved a close relative of Hope's.

Gene said that he was often asked to take an early train to New York to run errands for the Pelham Country Club golf shop, where he was an assistant. On the station platform Gene noticed that there were quite a few very pretty young women also going to the city at that early hour. Gene said that on several of these trips, he tried to strike up a conversation with one young woman that struck his fancy. He had no luck at all. It turned out that the girls were all dancers or singers in various Broadway shows and lived as roommates in Pelham, to avoid New York prices and rents.

"Ten years later," Gene said in the interview "I had just won the U.S. Open in Chicago and was on my way to the award ceremony when an official told me that there was a lady that would like to say a word to me."

"You don't recognize me, do you?" a very pretty lady said to Gene.

"No, I'm sorry I don't," replied Gene.

"You used to talk to me on the train platform years ago in Pelham," said the very pretty lady.

"I'm Mrs. Delores Hope." she went on. "I couldn't talk because I was engaged to Bob at the time, but I wanted to congratulate you on your win," said Mrs. Hope.

The Hopes have touched all of our lives in one way or another. As for Gene, however, who knows what would have happened had she decided to pursue the conversation on the train platform a bit further.

When I mentioned this incident to a friend of mine, Dick Harter, who also worked in the Time Inc. publishing halls at the same time, he had a Bob Hope story of his own.

Harter, now in the financial printing business, had stopped at a Texaco service station in Palm Springs and had gone into the station office with his driving companion for directions to a nearby golf course. At the time, Hope was doing his very successful weekly TV variety show, called the "Texaco Star Theatre."

When Harter and friend returned to the car, there was Bob Hope, the man, himself, pumping gas into their car.

"Well, who did you expect?" asked Hope.

As surprised as they were, the explanation was relatively simple.

Hope lived nearby and would often bring his own car to the station and on occasion would help out by manning the Texaco pumps for surprised and pleased patrons!

And, like Hope, it was much easier in those years to run into golf's stars in person. They had not yet reached the cocoon-like stage that agents now have them in.

I had never met Ben Hogan, but I had a near-miss in 1959. His schedule had taken him to Seminole at the same time *Sports Illustrated* had invited some guests to the club. He had just authored his well-known series of five instructional articles, "The Modern Fundamentals of Golf" for the magazine. Art Murphy, then *SI's* publisher, was at his locker area changing shoes when an attendant came around the corner.

"Mr. Murphy, there is a gentleman in the next aisle who would like to have a word with you," said the attendant.

Murphy was a tough Irishman from Boston who always knew what he was talking about at all times. And, he'd let you know it on occasion.

"Who is it?" asked Murphy.

"Mr. Ben Hogan," replied the attendant.

"Does Mr. Hogan want to talk golf or does he want to talk publishing?" asked Murphy.

"Publishing," answered the attendant.

"Fine, tell him to come over here." He turned to me and said, "If it was golf, I'd have gone over there!"

As it turned out, I was not there when they met later in the day, but I sure knew right then that I wanted to be a publisher someday.

Years later, when I was with *GOLF* Magazine, I was in the Hogan company offices in Fort Worth, Texas with Hank Rojas, the Hogan vice president for sales. Rojas was just about ready to introduce me to Mr. Hogan, but the great man was called out of the office to another meeting. I don't think that many people can say that they just missed meeting the legendary Hogan twice in one's career.

In 1960, under the theory that I could add up golf scores, someone put me in charge of that year's *Sports Illustrated* sales meeting golf tournament. Three celebrities were in attendance at Bermuda's Castle Harbour: Bill Russell of the Celtics, Bill Bradley, then studying at Oxford and John Galbreath, who then owned the Pittsburgh Pirates. Since I was theoretically in charge of the tournament, I decided to put the 14-handicap Bradley in my group. I had never met Bradley and I was in for several surprises.

Out on the course, Bradley's golf appeared to be somewhat lackadaisical. Since I thought our foursome might have a strong chance to win the tournament, I mentioned to Bradley that we could win a substantial amount of money if we all played our best.

"How much?" asked Bradley.

"$250 each," I replied.

Keep in mind that Bradley had not signed his "Dollar Bill" contract for the Knicks yet, and most college people were usually in need of some extra cash. As soon as an amount that large (for those years) was announced, he was a changed man. He started keeping the ball in play, often "laying up" short of trouble. His putting began to resemble the accuracy of his jump shots.

We won the tournament easily. You just have to tell a potential pro how much they are playing for!

Those wonderful days of corporate entertainment at that level may never be prevalent ever again. The effectiveness of those trips was best portrayed by a Madison avenue ad agency that held an early morning meeting to explain how various magazines were picked for the Gordon's Gin advertising schedule. The sales managers of *The New Yorker* and *Newsweek* were seated next to each other in the audience. At least 30 other magazines were represented that day and we all knew that only 10 magazines were actually selected for that given year. It was not a happy gathering.

The agency presenter ran through the initial list of publications and both *Newsweek* and *The New Yorker* were up on the screen. No *TIME* Magazine. A second list went up on the screen. Both magazines were still there. Still no *TIME*.

"Right about here," said Jack Mandable of *Newsweek*, "*TIME* Magazine opens the hangar doors", obviously referring to *TIME's* use of the F27 for various customer golf trips. He said it in a voice loud enough to be heard all over the room. In that instant on the screen, *Newsweek* disappeared and *TIME* appeared in its place. *The New Yorker* stayed and Bob Young, *The New Yorker's* ad director breathed more easily.

Gordon's Gin executives heard about the meeting and were not happy either. Making 40-some magazines upset with a Gordon's advertising decision could have cost the ad agency the business. As for *Newsweek* and *The New Yorker*, they probably spent the next two weeks looking for an F27!

One of the great media salesmen of that era was Jack Meyers of *TIME*. He went on to be Publisher of *TIME* and *Sports Illustrated* and later, chairman of *Time Inc.* According to those in attendance, Jack had received early one morning, a call from the *TIME* office in Detroit informing him that the Ford Motor Co. had taken great exception to an article that the editors had just written about Ford. Jack was told that they would cancel all of their advertising in *TIME*, a very sizeable number.

A decision was made to invite the top Ford marketing executive to Pine Valley, a course that he had always wanted to play. The man accepted and they sent the G2 to Detroit.

Meyers had never met the man from Detroit, but was paired with him on the first day of play. Nothing was said about the editorial piece in question, but Meyers had already engaged the client in conversation on the very first hole. As they walked down the second fairway, the client could be seen laughing with Jack. In fact, Jack had his arm over the client's shoulder.

Later, in the clubhouse it was readily apparent that Ford and *TIME* were no longer at odds. One of the other *TIME* executives commented that, "Meyers seems to be losing his touch with clients. It took him until the second hole before he fixed the situation."

The day held one more surprise before it was over. Going back to Westchester airport in the company helicopter, (which was shared by the Rockefeller Foundation), the chopper made an additional stop at the 59th Street heliport to "pick someone up" according to the pilots. Onto the helicopter stepped the then Vice President of the United States, Nelson Rockefeller. When Rockefeller, dressed in a business suit, spotted the passenger compartment filled with tired men in golf clothing, he said, "It looks like you gentlemen had a better day than I did." Indeed.

It is likely that none of these events could take place in today's commodity pricing culture. All advertising, as well as most corporate purchases, are now made on a computer, with very little interface with any representatives from either the selling company or from the purchasing company. Client entertainment, if there is any at all, has now taken a different form. Much of it, if it is done at all, is on a wider scale in an "event" format like a movie or a concert.

There is also something else to be noted about the disappearance of face-to-face meetings with a client. Now missing in this computer ambiance is the trust that personal contact once generated. Far too many executives are hiding behind the isolating wall of less and less contact with outsiders.

In many cases, the isolation is intentional, requiring little oversight and even less obligation. We could do no worse as a society if we just rolled out the old F27 again.

LUNCH

CHAPTER 4

SUMMER. WORLDWIDE.

I always thought that one of the best parts of golf was lunch, and on occasion, a golf dinner. To my knowledge no one has yet given lunch its own chapter in a book. Golf is played either before lunch or after lunch. And I decided that if I were ever to write a book involving the game, one of the chapters was going to be on, perhaps, the most important ritual ever invented for any sport. There is a strong case to be made that lunch is far more important to golf than the game itself.

If you really give some serious thought to golf lunches, anywhere, anytime, you'll probably agree that it is an activity that carries right over to most of life as well. Lunch could very well be the last place on earth where one can spend two hours with a customer, an activity that many corporations will still pay for. If the CFO added up all of the revenue his or her salespeople brought in over lunch, I think it could certainly add up to well over 50% of the corporation's total volume.

Here's your basic club foursome either at lunch or on the course.

Person #1 has some kind of clout.

Person #2 wants something from Person #1.

Persons #3 is usually a fairly good golfer, and #4 can be just about anybody, just as long as they can tell a great joke or nod appreciatively.

Most luncheon conversations are led by (#1) Al Del Granite, President of Mid-Town Construction. Del Granite has a thousand and one new ideas for building yet another 60-story edifice, several of which might actually work.

Person (#2) is Ted Wordsworthy, a top executive at a recently hot advertising agency. Ted set up the game and would dearly like to get his hands on one of Del Granite's projects for the agency.

The golfing part of the conversation is led by person (#3), Adrian Tourister, who took back his amateur status two years ago and is now in the shipping business. All necessary adulation is given Adrian on the course. But, once back in the clubhouse, Adrian stops talking and Del Granite resumes describing his plan for organizing condominiums on the Throg's Neck Bridge.

It was this way even in prehistoric times, with the best archer getting attention until the fire was lit. As the fire grew, all conversation turned back to the tribal leader, who wasn't much of a shot, but who could usually buy everybody else out.

Danny McGowan, a very successful manufacturer's rep, was always a great # 4, beloved by all members, i.e. mostly male. Few females could be given too many details to many of his stories. Nevertheless, Danny, or someone like him was welcome everywhere, every time, in any men's grille. Should someone try to get political or even head toward an argument, the Dannys' of the world deftly solved the problem with what always seems to be the perfect comment or story.

Here's a reported description of a conversation between a "Danny" in his Detroit office and his new boss in New York. In this case, the "Danny" was one Fred Cody, manager of the old *Look* Magazine office in that city. His brother, Burns Cody, was an even better-known character in Detroit advertising circles and was the arch-rival *LIFE* Magazine manager.

The conversation with New York went roughly as follows: "Fred, I'd like to come out to Detroit and visit several of our top customers, particularly the new advertising director at Goodyear in Akron." says the New York boss.

Fred is not happy with the intrusion, but agrees to the visit. Before he hangs up, Fred warns the boss in New York that, "The man at Goodyear is hard of hearing." "You have to speak loudly enough for him to hear."

"OK, thanks," says New York.

Fred hangs up on New York and next gets Akron on the phone, "Would you have a chance to see my new boss from New York in the next two weeks?"

"Sure, no problem," says Goodyear.

"Great," says Fred. "But, just remember that my boss from New York is hard of hearing. You have to speak loudly enough for him to hear."

The great day arrived and both men exchanged greetings in the client's office in Akron.

"HELLO, HOW ARE YOU?" demanded NY.

"FINE. HOW ARE YOU?" responded Goodyear.

"Why are you shouting at each other?" asked Fred.

Obviously, neither man had a hearing problem. The three of them went off to a very funny, successful luncheon.

Regardless of who fills in the #4 spot or what story is told, lunch can be critical to moving almost any piece of business toward the goal line. In fact, it would have helped Martha Burk to be included in one of those lunches at Augusta National. Danny would have held up on the men-only stories, but at least she would have started from the "inside" rather than from the "outside."

Some golf lunches have surprise endings. The one that I have in mind involves a delightful boss of mine at *TIME* in the '70's, Jack Higgons. "Higgo" always liked lunch with a customer, but he often asked for so much detail in preparing for the guest that we all learned to get him involved at the last minute. The fact was that he was often much better in a sales situation unprepared than prepared!

The situation we found ourselves in was that the customer was in the automotive business and shared with us an advertising plan put together by his ad agency. The basic plan was a full-page ad in both *Newsweek* and *U.S. News* once every month and a single page in *Business Week*. No one could figure out a reason for the single page in *Business Week*.

Higgo said that he could find two problems with the agency's proposal.

"First, it has a single page in *Business Week*", assessed Higgo. He followed up by saying, "Second, there is no *TIME* Magazine on the list."

The customer replied, "What do you think I should do?"

Only Higgo could come up with the next comment, "*TIME* can waste your money more effectively."

Within days *Business Week* was gone and *TIME* ended up with the same schedule as *Newsweek* and *U.S. News*.

There is a magic to most lunches and particularly golf lunches, that golfers will know about and non-golfers won't. In every golf foursome, there is a clear understanding between the players that they will be together all day. That bond, in itself, creates a strong understanding and in most cases, avoids ruffling feathers. Think about that. Golf, particularly, is a business game and almost guarantees comity. Maybe our State Department should put together a golf team.

Almost with this in mind, over the years, *Time Inc.* magazines would throw several industry-related meetings during a given year always in tandem with a golf outing and an outstanding luncheon. But, what would be key to these meetings would be to invite an advertiser to be the guest speaker at the ensuing luncheon. It cemented many an industry relationship and eventually turned us all into damned good friends.

On occasion, something out of the ordinary will pop up. One Winged Foot luncheon conversation involved some very successful club members who had just finished a closely-contested $2.00

Nassau bet. They were abruptly interrupted by a man from an adjoining table who wanted to know if he could be part of their new business consortium.

"I'd love to be involved," said the intruder.

"Well, the initial investment is quite high – one million dollars," was the response.

"Well, I've made a modest amount of money in my lifetime," said the intruder.

Clearly annoyed at the intrusion, one of the other golfers asked, "How much is that?"

"$15 million," was the reply.

"Oh, that is a modest amount of money!" came the even-faster reply.

In years gone by, Winged Foot had a table next to the center window in its grille that had some of the most famous golfers in the world having lunch together. Craig Wood, Claude Harmon, Mike Souchak, Tommy Armour and Dave Marr to name a few that were at that table daily. If you were patient and built a reputation for asking reasonably intelligent questions, in time, you would be invited to join them. But it was always their nickel, not yours. And you could always hear an apocryphal story that could only come from the ranks of great players. Whether it actually happened or not is almost of no importance.

Here's one involving Scotland and Armour. According to lunch table chatter, Tommy had a blind shot over a hill. He turned to his caddy and asked for the line to the green. The caddy pointed to a mast on a ship just visible over the brow of the hill.

What the caddy did not know was that Armour had been gassed in World War I and one of the results was that he could not focus his eyes immediately on the ball. On this occasion, Armour took an inordinate number of waggles (13) before he hit his shot. He finally hit the ball and walked over the hill only to find that the ball was not in the fairway, and was, in fact, in deep rough. Upset, Armour questioned the offending caddy and demanded an explanation.

"Aye sir, but you have to hit the ball before the ship puts out to sea!" came the answer.

Along the way at that table, one could certainly learn some critical things about how top golfers approach the game, but in an equal number of cases, these same great players were as interested in the business you represented as they were in their own. Maybe more. Both Claude Harmon and Craig Wood ended up associated with area automobile dealerships as a result of their close association with several of the members. In more recent years we have all watched players like Greg Norman or Ben Crenshaw go on from the game to success in the business world. Incidentally, both men were on the *GOLF* Magazine playing staff in the 1980s and had terrific "touch" with the magazine's customers.

In fact, one of the most thoughtful things I've ever seen happen in the game occurred at a *GOLF* Magazine outing at Greenwich, Connecticut's Stanwich Club in September 1984. Ben Crenshaw had just won the Masters that April, a victory that is still one of the most admired major championship victories ever. The editor of *GOLF* Magazine had annually written a beautifully illustrated text and photo account of all four rounds of each year's Masters for the club. As the eventual winner of that year's Masters, photos of Crenshaw were predominant.

Ben was the guest professional that day at Stanwich. During cocktails, our editor announced that several boxes of that year's Master's books had just come off the press and had been delivered to the club. Since it was late in the afternoon, the editor asked Ben if he would mind signing a few copies. Ben probably had a dinner engagement, but stayed late anyway, signing every book for every guest. He included an individual and different note for each guest's book. There were two dozen guests.

You never saw people so proud to get such a gift. One man called me up the next day and said, "He was up all night going down to his living room to keep looking at the book and his inscription from Ben."

Ben really is that thoughtful, as the whole golfing world saw in his role as winning Ryder Cup Captain at Brookline in 1999, as well as throughout his career, both as an amateur and professional.

Often, equally serious to the guests in attendance at a golf luncheon, is the menu itself. Joe McMahon, a long-time successful New York City executive search expert would come through the men's locker room door at Winged Foot on any given Saturday and be greeted with a Heineken's as he changed his shoes. Next, he headed up the stairs into the grille room where he was served a stem

Martini. That was followed by a medium rare cheeseburger.

Joe had been a scratch player 40 years ago at Northwestern and his game, even as he put some years on, remained reasonably sharp. Joe attributed his lasting skill level to the "warm-up" that he had perfected over the years. It might not work for everybody, but why fix it if it ain't broke?

Drinks were equally as personal as the people involved. Armour, for example, would religiously stop at the bar half-way through a round and get what he called a "gin buck;" in this case, a mixture of gin and Alka-Seltzer. Not too light on the gin. Others took equally exotic drinks with them out to the course at the turn. Always in a plastic cup that no one questioned. It is probably to the plus side that considerably less alcohol goes along with golf these days, but there was a time when "aiming fluid" was quite prevalent among friends and just plain social golfers. Sometimes I miss those days.

And before we leave the subject of golf lunches, most of them take place in some of the most beautiful rooms in the world or overlook a vista that is incomparable. Few settings can compare to having lunch on the porch at Brookline next to the famous 18th green where so much golf history has taken place over the years. Ditto for Merion's porch next to the first tee or Oakmont's view down 18. Add Eastward Ho's stretch of ocean on the Cape. And put Cypress Point on the list.

Anyone that has been to Pine Valley knows that the dining room has an unmatched menu and an ambiance that few restaurants in the world have, including Cipriani's out on its own island in Venice.

And, you'd better mark down Shinnecock's porch with its sweeping view down its 18th fairway, and for the granddaddy of them all, don't miss the cold half-lobsters on the screened porch overlooking Long Island Sound at the National Golf Links of America next door to Shinnecock.

The remarkable thing about golf's luncheon rooms, regardless of where we all go in the world, is that we can make up our own list of equally memorable locations and one list is usually better than the next. Throw in the fact that there's always an Umberto and Caesar, or a Ralph or Eddie, or a "Big Ed", who not only knows you, but who will go out of their way to make you and your guests comfortable and welcome.

In the final analysis, regardless of setting, perhaps the most important ingredient in any foursome or luncheon meeting is "reading" the real wishes of each of the participants.

Go to any bookstore and you can find various sales "experts" who are writing books about how to play golf with a client. You can save yourself some money if you just listen carefully. You'll find that any "next step" will be clearly spelled out somewhere along the way during the day. The real trick is to get into the foursome in the first place. As one sage said, "Showing up is 90% of success."

Today's "hard-nosed" approach to business, including those dreaded "power" breakfasts, don't come close to what can get done in an hour and a half lunch before or after golf. "In your face selling" at any level simply makes people uneasy and looking for the door. And it always takes the next corporate management team to find out how much the customers actually resented being bullied.

Lunch at a golf club, even today, still provides a setting for understanding and rapport that can last for a very, very long time. Problems big and small are settled. You can even find out what $15 million is really worth, if the subject is not handled properly!

You'll also meet some unforgettable characters. Albeit somewhat less these days, but nevertheless, there are still enough around to make things interesting.

And, most of them can help you immeasurably somewhere along the line in a myriad of activities.

MIKE MANUCHE'S

CHAPTER 5

W. 52ND ST., NYC, APRIL 1960

*M*ike Manuche opened his first Manhattan restaurant in 1948 on 2nd Avenue and 51st Street. Mike knew then that Time Inc. and CBS would soon be the first large organizations moving to Sixth Avenue to be followed by many other corporations seeking the new buildings that the West Side was offering. His neighboring restaurateurs all cautioned him to stay on the East Side of town. Instead, Mike made the move to the West Side in 1960. It was a brilliant move.

The new Manuche's was on 52nd St. between 6th and 7th Avenues near Rockefeller Center. It quickly became the weekday gathering spot for every golfer, storyteller and athlete in New York City and on many occasions, probably in the country. Virtually every media salesman was found there, always with a customer or two. It was busy from just before lunch to well past midnight. Well-known golfers and equally well-known athletes dotted the dining areas and the bar.

~~~~~~~~~~

Mike had been a football player at Holy Cross in the 1940's and it was natural for him to attract other athletes. He was also a member at Winged Foot. At the new restaurant, it became commonplace to see the greats from almost any sport one could imagine. In the early '60s, Arnold Palmer was spotted at a table watching a 14-handicap bar patron demonstrating a chip shot to another bar patron.

With the King watching the demonstration, the 14-handicap casually turned toward Arnold and announced that "he'd get to him in a minute, just as soon as he finished with his lesson at the bar." He also added that he thought Palmer was "a bit quick on his takeaway."

Claude Harmon, Winged Foot professional and the 1948 Masters champion, would hold court at dinner on many a Wednesday evening at Mike's. He would take his rapt listeners through shot after shot of every major tournament he ever played in. Unknown to Claude, Mike Souchak, one of Claude's many great assistants provided a bit of knowledge that not many knew at the time.

Souchak explained that, in every conversation about one of Harmon's competitive rounds, "Claude always changed the club, the shot, and the circumstances every time he described a tournament shot." Mike added, "The score was always correct because you could look it up."

Mike explained further that "Claude just got bored telling people over and over again how his shots were actually hit."

Anyone needing an explanation of where Claude's sons got their golfing expertise, need only note what Hogan said about Claude, "He knows as much about the golf swing as anybody that ever lived."

Customers and athletes mixed freely and no one was left unscathed in Manuche's. Many of the championship New York

Giants spent off-hours in Mike's. The walls of the restaurant had many paintings of contemporary Giant stars. Alex Webster, the great Giant fullback, who never dropped the ball, had fumbled on the previous Sunday, and he was about to hear about it all over again.

"Alex, you gotta take better care of the ball! You're killing me!" nagged one of the restaurant's faithful and obvious game-day bettors.

In those days, the expense account made things tick. Mike had an accountant named Ira Weinman who kept after the many corporate customers who received expense checks once a month. Weinman would, on occasion, get on the phone and call a customer or two inquiring as to when an overdue bill could be expected.

One who received a call from Ira was an original *Sports Illustrated* advertising salesman, Bob Kerrigan. On one occasion, somewhat frustrated by Ira's persistence, Kerrigan demanded, "Ira, do you have any idea how I pay my bills?"

You could tell by Kerrigan's impatience that Ira answered, "No." Kerrigan explained to Ira that, "once a month I put all of my bills in a hat. "And once a month, I pull out ten of those bills and pay them."

Before Ira could offer a word, Kerrigan said, "Ira, if you don't get off my back, I'm not even going to put your bill in my hat!"

Mike recalled many years after the incident that he had to speak to Ira after that encounter with Kerrigan. The bills always, eventually, got paid.

While expense accounts were the order of the day, corporate

management was also vigilant in staying on top of the sales staff's spending. One delightful and competent *Sports Illustrated* business manager named Peter Hanson, all 6'-8" of him, asked a staff salesman, David Benford, about his expenditures at Manuche's. By way of answering the question, Benford invited Peter to a hockey game with some of his customers. Peter, not used to having cocktails at 5:30 p.m. indicated to Benford sometime before dinner that he would, in fact, like to skip the hockey game and go on home to Connecticut. Peter wished everyone a good evening and to a man, they all understood.

It's also fair to say that Peter never asked another question about sales expenditures at Manuche's.

Not all physical activity in Manuche's was limited to the Giants in those days. The only better arm wrestler in the East, other than Mike himself, might have been George, the head bartender. Perhaps the most spectacular session occurred late one afternoon when a slightly built Texan sidled up to Mike and invited him to arm wrestle for $2,500. Serious stuff. Mike had a habit of greeting a new customer by putting his hand on his back. Most people thought that Mike was simply being friendly. What Mike was actually doing was getting an idea of how strong the customer was in case there was to be some arm wrestling.

Mike found absolutely no muscular structure on the Texan whatsoever. Mike concluded that the man had to know a trick or two about the sport.

After getting the rules and the bet settled, George counted

to "three." Mike threw every ounce of strength in his right arm into his first move. The next thing George and Mike saw was the Texan's two legs straight in the air. His head had hit the lower bar railing and Mike and George thought the man was dead. Fortunately, within a few minutes the man regained his senses, immediately paid his bet off, and politely left the premises. Mike had just about forgotten the incident when three months later the Texan reappeared at the bar.

He greeted Mike warmly and then asked, "Can we do that again, this time left-handed?" George simply shook his head.

Every one of these 52nd Street saloons had their own share of personalities. Toots Shors was a DiMaggio hangout. Toots loved to have athletes and celebrities in his restaurant. Toots once made a bet with Jackie Gleason that he could beat Jackie running around the block of 51st and 52nd streets, between 5th and 6th Avenues. Jackie easily beat Toots. In fact, he was waiting in the lobby of the restaurant when Toots finally came in.

It was only when Toots realized that he had not passed or seen Jackie on the street since they had gone in opposite directions, that Jackie finally owned up to the fact that he had hailed a cab for the race!

Just off 7th Avenue was, and still is, Gallagher's, another of the great West Side gathering spots. The second-floor dining room at Gallagher's was often the site for the annual *TIME*-Phillip Morris Christmas party. Probably one hundred marketing and advertising people attended each year. Dick Maylander, the *TIME* rep on the account was the one that came up with the idea for getting together with the Phillip Morris executives.

The 1976 party, on the occasion of our nation's 200th Anniversary, was to have a motif that would have several of the *TIME* people dressed in the military uniforms of the Revolutionary era. Rob Mountain, now in the financial business, was the "rookie" on the downstairs door complete with musket, uniform and tri-corner hat.

The speaker's table for the evening was set on a stage. On the table was a small Revolutionary style cannon that could shoot a one-inch iron ball a very considerable distance. The cannon was aimed at a blank wall at the side of the room. Maylander took center stage and armed the firing mechanism. Some say that the cannon fired against the wall. Others say it didn't. In any event, all of the guests felt that the evening got off to splendid start.

No one ever asked Maylander if he put a hole in the wall on his expense account!

Maylander's parties would rival any thrown by Fifth Avenue dignitaries. The gathering that may go down in history is the one he threw for, yes, the horse, Secretariat, the year it won the Triple Crown in 1973. *TIME* Magazine put the thoroughbred on the cover as "Horse of the Year." By coincidence, the back cover had another horse in the form of White Horse Scotch, a company owned by Phillip Morris. Maylander decided to present both covers to Phillip Morris at that year's Christmas gala.

At the same time, he also got the idea to invite Penny Tweedy, the owner of Secretariat. To everyone's surprise, Penny said she loved parties and accepted. Maylander next got the idea to invite the horse, himself, which Penny declined. She did agree to bring his silks, however.

Maylander then called the New York police stables, still located in Central Park. They said they not only had a horse that had Secretariat's markings, but they would be glad to bring the horse to the Landmark Tavern, which was, and still is, on 46th St. and 11th Avenue. You can imagine the traffic watching the world famous horse heading down 11th Avenue. The only problem was that the horse balked at the entrance and had to stay outside for the duration of the party. It was a small price to pay for one of the great soirees of the year. In fact, a major movie was just recently released recounting all of the events, not including the Maylander party of course, that developed during the horse's monumental year.

One fall evening in the seventies, a number of *Sports Illustrated* customers had gathered at Gallagher's to go by chartered bus on to the Ali-Zora Folley championship bout at the Garden. At the end of the bar, a large handsome man in his mid-30s, dressed in an expensive camel's hair top coat stood drinking a beer with a very attractive blond. It was hard to miss the pair.

Eventually the *SI* dinner group made its way to the Garden to watch the preliminaries. They were just getting settled in their seats when someone noticed that the large man in the camel's hair coat from the bar had not only come to the Garden, but was now in boxing trunks in the ring matched up in the second preliminary fight.

It was quickly apparent that he could handle himself in the ring and was much better than his opponent. But at the end of the second round something went very wrong and he found himself losing in a TKO. Several hours later we all went back to Gallagher's and were stunned to find a very unscathed "camels hair coat" fighter back at the bar with his lovely companion. The fighter explained that he saw no particular reason, including financial, to stay in the fight any longer than necessary since the amount of money wouldn't change, even if it went the full four rounds!

Nobody ever said that the prelims required strenuous training.

"21" was another stop on the trek across 52nd Street. At 6 p.m. the bar was three deep with CBS, ABC and Time Inc. sales personnel. As one sales executive pointed out, "You're not going to find out what's going in the business world sitting in your office."

You could find many show business characters in the bar area at "21" including at least on one occasion, Kirk Douglas and Frank Sinatra having dinner with their wives right next to the bar. Alan King often stopped off to be with the regulars and try out a few new lines on the assemblage. *TIME* Magazine added Associate Publisher, Lane Fortinberry, to the group by his appearance at "21" nearly every day for both lunch and dinner for several years running. He was given the nickname, "Old No. 42," by the magazine's business department and the nickname is now engraved on a nameplate in today's bar area in memory of his name and stick-to-itiveness.

Even John Wayne made a late-morning appearance at the "21" bar. Jack Keefe, a veteran *Time* salesman was in charge of a luncheon advertising meeting at "21." In the few minutes he had before the meeting upstairs started, Jack went to the bar downstairs for a soft drink. He was suddenly confronted by the large figure of an unmistakable John Wayne.

"The Duke," the only other person at the bar, explained to a totally surprised Keefe, that "he had to get to the bar early if he was going to get a drink since no one in his luncheon group drank at all."

Next to "21" which is still in business under a different name, was Rose's Restaurant on the ground floor of the CBS building. "Mama" Rose and son Buzzy Buzzalino, oversaw each evening's crowd with great care and service. Many media salesmen from all the networks and big magazines were always at the bar.

Jack Purcell, who oversaw the CBS publishing group, had just finished an afternoon board meeting at CBS. William Paley was in attendance. As the meeting wound down, members were invited to stay for cocktails. Purcell told a number of the participants that he was going downstairs to Rose's where he could pick up the most recent and pertinent information in the industry all in one room. That's exactly how information was transported in those days. You didn't even have to wait for the "trades" to come out a few days later.

With all this activity on the West Side, there was only one critical watering hole on the East Side, and that was P. J. Clarke's.

Like Manuche's and the rest of the restaurants, you could run into most everybody from the media end of the business at one time or another in the early evening. But, on many occasions, it was the last stop for the night. Late one evening at Clarke's, a young Time Inc., businessman was asked by his boss as to where he'd like his career to take him. It is a serious question and one that should be asked and answered seriously – but probably not late at night.

Even so, the young businessman gave some thought to this momentous question and replied: "What I'd really like to do is get across Fifth Avenue by midnight!"

Jack Whitaker, the famous television sports announcer and commentator was, of course, known for his articulate wrap-ups of some of the most famous sporting events, not the least of which was the Kentucky Derby. After a chilly mid-April round of golf as Jack's guest at Shinnecock, we ended up in a local watering hole in Watermill for a casual dinner. The television was tuned to a two-hour special on American fighter planes going against Libya and Moammar Gadhafi, of all people. As the program droned on, various patrons, perhaps prompted by strong beverage, began to talk over the broadcast, announcing their own descriptions of the events on the screen.

"Look at this, the guy can't fight," announced one viewer in a voice imitating John Madden.

"The rockets are coming straight in," cried the ersatz Madden. "He's got his sandbags all stacked too far to the right."

The neighborhood's Mike Francessa exclaimed, "Gadhafi seems

to be in over his head."

As the broadcast was coming to an end, Whitaker himself took over, "Well, there you have it, ladies and gentlemen. It was a good fight, not a great fight.

"We'll look forward to the next two hour special in August brought to you by Lockheed and Grumman," continued Whitaker.

Sitting at a table alone was a very amused Gwen Verdon, the famous Broadway dancer. Everybody went home with a smile on their face.

In the final analysis, the IRS killed the expense accounts. And, along with expense money went a lot of the "social cement" that prevailed in an admittedly male oriented society. To say nothing about the number of key restaurant jobs that were lost in the process.

There is always some lament and nostalgia when an era passes. I had the opportunity to play a summer round of golf in 1984 at Westhampton with Frank Barry who owned the Circle Line. Part of the fairway conversation turned to the changing nature of current American business.

Barry surveyed the shifting social scene and noted "I think we've seen the best of it!"

But there did remain one bright spot that stayed open for the sports and late-night crowd and that was the Four Seasons bar in the Seagram's building. From the mid-'80s and for the next 15 years, Henry Mielke and Jim Kelly, two of the best bartenders in town, kept many well-known businessmen and athletes, including

Mike Tyson, in a comfortable ambiance in one of the city's most popular restaurants.

In actuality, today's major bar scene has moved further south in the city with a totally different generation taking over the early night in New York. Similar switches in location have taken place in city after city across the nation.

Indeed, as one looks back it is now easy to see that business, itself, was something that was becoming mistrusted. And long before the Bernie Madoffs' of the world starting making headlines, entertainment and expense accounts were already getting a bad name. It was the end of many of the great mid-town oases.

They just shut their doors and went away, quietly and sadly.

SHOW BUSINESS

CHAPTER 6

BAY HILL CLUB, ORLANDO, FLORIDA, AUGUST 24, 1995

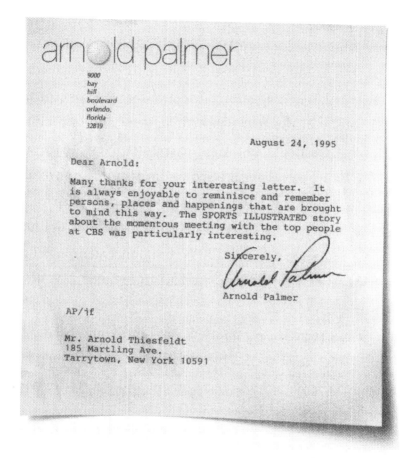

arnold palmer

9000
bay
hill
boulevard
orlando,
florida
32819

August 24, 1995

Dear Arnold:

Many thanks for your interesting letter. It is always enjoyable to reminisce and remember persons, places and happenings that are brought to mind this way. The SPORTS ILLUSTRATED story about the momentous meeting with the top people at CBS was particularly interesting.

Sincerely,

Arnold Palmer

AP/jf

Mr. Arnold Thiesfeldt
185 Martling Ave.
Tarrytown, New York 10591

Palmer's letter herein refers to *Sports Illustrated's* decision to move its weekly closing date from Friday night to Sunday evening and CBS's decision to go to a full schedule of sports activities over the weekends.

Since CBS began televising the Masters in 1956, some of the most unlikely broadcasting venues have developed into major forces in sport and in golf.

Twenty three years later in 1978, a 45-year-old Bill Rasmussen left his job as communications director of the Hartford Whalers and decided that if you could convince local area teams to air their games on cable television and call it ESPN, you might just have something that could be successful. Not many people agreed.

The critics all presented strong evidence that the concept would not work at all. In the first place, there were only a total of 14 million cable subscribers, in the entire country. Next, they pointed out that he didn't even have a building in Bristol, Connecticut to broadcast from and had to use trailer trucks for office space. They also said he had to lease something called a satellite "uplink." In fact, at Rasmussen's original ESPN announcement meeting at a Holiday Inn in Connecticut, he had the grand total of three reporters in the audience.

Most people were simply amused that cable could be any factor at all in the broadcast world. Nevertheless, it was not long before they changed the name to Entertainment and Sports Network. A year later in 1979, absolutely nobody was laughing when Getty Oil saw the eventual potential involved and paid Rasmussen $10 million for 85% of his venture! Today, ESPN has several different channels available to millions of viewers including their all sports update channel called "Sports Center." ESPN now broadcasts 65 sports, 24-hours a day, in 16 languages in more than 200 countries.

In 1996 the Walt Disney companies purchased Capital Cities/ABC for $19 billion and picked up an 80% stake in ESPN at that time. According to an analysis published by *Barron's Magazine* in February 2008, ESPN is probably worth more than 40% of Disney's entire value.

While all this was going on at ESPN, in 1995 Arnold Palmer and television cable entrepreneur Joseph E. Gibbs of Birmingham, Alabama, put together a 24-hour television channel. It was called "The Golf Channel" and again, early critics similarly thought it could not succeed. With a 24-hour format, the thinking was that they would often duplicate their own coverage. Indeed, the early years were somewhat thin with infomercials and low-budget programming.

While Palmer and Gibbs are no longer directly involved with the company, Golf Channel's growth has been spectacular and today, more than 120 million homes around world have access to Golf Channel. And keep in mind these are "high-end" viewers attracting advertisers like Accenture, Mercedes, Coca Cola, IBM and Nationwide Insurance.

In February of 2011, Comcast, out of Philadelphia, the largest cable operator in the nation and the current owner of Golf Channel, acquired majority stake in NBC Universal from General Electric . As part of the acquisition, Golf Channel has now become part of the NBC Sports Group which now consists of NBC Sports, Golf Channel, VERSUS, and Comcast SportsNets. In 2007 the network embarked on a 15-year agreement to be the exclusive cable home for the PGA TOUR and in 2009, Golf Channel signed a 10-year agreement to be the LPGA's exclusive cable network.

As a practical matter, Golf Channel, with several notable exceptions, is now dominating weekly televised golf. As early as 1997, its signal went into Canada and from there into the Caribbean, the United Kingdom, Middle East, Hong Kong, Korea and Scandinavia with plans for even more countries in the immediate future.

Not bad for something that "had no chance!"

Today, with networks intermingling with each other, a viewer can become confused as to whose corporate camera he or she is watching in a given tournament. For example, during Masters week, ESPN broadcast the Thursday and Friday's rounds, while CBS did the weekends. CBS did the PGA on the weekend and TNT did the weekdays. For the U.S. Open, NBC did Saturday and Sunday while ESPN did Thursday and Friday. In addition to its contracts with the LPGA and the PGA TOUR, Golf Channel has additional contracts with the Nationwide Tour and the Champions' Tour as well.

It is also worth noting that the actual broadcast from a golf course started with 30 to 40 technicians and staff working Saturday and Sunday afternoon, four holes on the back nine only. In fact, Clifford Roberts in his book *The Story of Augusta National Golf Club*, writes that the first telecast of the Masters had a one-hour show on Friday, April 6, with one hour on Saturday and Sunday each. Holes 15, 16, 17 and 18 were covered by seven cameras. Three more cameras were added for Sunday.

In the current broadcast format, a major tournament staff could number as many as 400 or more working not only on the event itself, but also many additional hours in recapitulation of those same events. Instead of two afternoons, all four tournament days are now televised.

Mark Loomis, son of well-known *Fortune* Magazine financial editor, Carol Loomis, headed up the most recent ABC golf group as coordinating producer. Loomis oversaw some 50 golf broadcast personnel and added 50 local technicians to each broadcast as they went from tournament to tournament. Now that ABC has turned its golf over to ESPN, Loomis has moved to ESPN.

You can now find a corporate sponsor for almost every tournament imaginable. There are commercials with quacking ducks, geckos, dogs and bees marching across the commercial screen. And much of it is all aimed at an older market which seems antithetical to the perceived needs of today's young media buyers.

Incredibly, the ad game still wants younger viewers and readers even as the overwhelming purchasing strengths of well-to-do Baby Boomers are often ignored. Here is a vast market of very wealthy people, including golfers that own everything from stocks and bonds and whiskey, from Mercedes and Jaguars, to second homes and memberships in golf clubs.

What is particularly fascinating is that while all of the current television coverage and tournament activities proceed with almost no limits, golfers are obviously playing fewer rounds each year. With the exception of the Masters, few tournaments get a national rating of more than a five share, which translates to about a million homes per rating point. That doesn't even match the number of "avid" golfers in the entire country!

One conclusion is that watching golf is more of a sport than playing it is. Another conclusion is that unless Tiger Woods or someone of his celebrity is in the hunt, far too many viewers fail to tune in. The other problem is a bit more insidious. When a Tiger or Rory McIlroy does play, many of the viewers are too often curious spectators and, as such, are not in the market for golf equipment.

Further, many of the ex-players who do the commentary often interject their own playing experience into the assessment of tournament events. Some of it can be intrusive, even silly, particularly when discussing a negative that has occurred to a leading player. Thankfully, many like Golf Channel's Brandel Chamblee, Rich Lerner and Frank Nobilo have things in balance and are quite interesting to listen to on the air. Add a knowledgeable female in Kelly Tilghman and a venerable golf reporter, Tim Rosaforte, and it all works.

Still, after all these seasons, Johnny Miller is often openly critical of a player's shot-making abilities. Although lately, Miller seems to be somewhat more forgiving when it comes to his on-air remarks.

Here's golf's all time classic on-course reporting from an ex-player, the late Bob Rosburg, a number of years back, in describing an upcoming shot by Jack Nicklaus.

"Oh, he's got a terrible lie here. He's got no chance to get to the green." opines Rosburg.

Cut to the shot.

"Well, he's got a birdie putt now," says the lead announcer, the incomparable Dave Marr.

Galleries themselves have changed. For example, the U.S. Open came to Winged Foot for the fifth time in 2006 and attracted 40,000 people each day in the galleries. What a difference from the Open at Winged Foot in 1929 when Bob Jones played in front of a gallery that was allowed to walk many of the fairways along with the players. It was a stroll in the park.

The number of people going to a tournament today has reached as high as 45,000, as they did for the Ryder Cup at Brookline in 1999. The British Open has galleries that are even larger each year, with upwards of 50,000 in attendance. With a crowd that large it is almost impossible to get views of play unless one stations oneself all day long at a single location. In 2006, Winged Foot had a total of 72 hospitality tents and a USGA brochure pointed out that the only way to have access to a block of tickets to the Open was to purchase a tent for the week.

A typical tent a few years ago could run into the many hundreds of thousands of dollars, complete with lunches, drinks and in some cases, both breakfast and dinner. Add in travel, prizes and trips and a total of close to a million dollars could be the result.

It is entirely possible that a spectator could stay in a hospitality tent all week long and watch the events going on outside the tent on a television screen next to a nearby refreshment bar. Many did just that and never went near the course for the entire week.

However, with a slowing economy, the number of tents sold has been cut back, as has the number of sponsors. For example, the automotive industry has slowed down on large-scale promotions. Financial services have been forced to pull back. Insurance companies are still making appearances, but have also been affected by business uncertainties.

Hopefully, the field won't get as spare as it was for the 1959 U.S. Open at Winged Foot. For that event, the *Sports Illustrated* sales staff was allowed to place one of the few entertainment tents at the tournament immediately next to the 15th green on the West Course. It was on the lot immediately to right of golf impresario Fred Corcoran's home. By today's standards, having a single entertainment tent on one particular hole seems out of touch with reality.

Advertising sales guests back then were no different than those of today when it came to entertainment. They wanted to have a good time and they could get loud. As the noise level rose in the *Sports Illustrated* tent at the 1959 U.S. Open, 1958 U.S. Open champion Tommy Bolt, trying to putt on the 15th green just outside the tent, became irate at a woman yelling for her husband, Harry, to "get her a gin and tonic."

Bolt marched off the 15th green, around the trap, and into the doorway of the tent. He confronted a very surprised group of party enthusiasts and demanded, "For God's sake, Harry, get her a gin and tonic so I can get on with the U.S. Open!" That was undoubtedly the last time a tent was allowed that close to the playing area.

Speaking of Fred Corcoran, Fred became one of my sponsors for membership at Winged Foot in 1967. I was introduced to Fred by *SI's* then-managing editor, Sid James. Sid was working with both Fred and Jim Linen, Time Inc.'s president, putting together the Canada Cup, which Fred had help start in 1955. In order to widen its base and appeal, the event was given a new name, also in 1967, calling it the World Cup. The annual contest sent a two-man team from the U.S. to play against other two man teams from various countries around the world. In various forms and venues, the event continues to this day.

Two weeks before Fred died in 1977, he mentioned that we had never played golf together at the club. He suggested that as soon as he returned from a trip to the mid-west we would do so. We never got the chance. When something good is on your schedule, do it right then!

On the occasion of the 75th Anniversary of Winged Foot's founding in 1923, the club made the decision to hold a major celebration complete with an entertainment tent of its own that included member Jim Nantz as the master of ceremonies and Peter Duchin as the bandleader for the evening's festivities. Billy Morley, a former board member was asked to be the program chairman. Billy thought that the evening's activities might benefit greatly by inviting the past Open winners back to the occasion.

Billy was certainly prepared to pay for certain legitimate expenses for the several past winners, but what he was surprised at was the insistent demand from several of them for a sizeable "appearance fee." Without a payment, they would not attend, even though it was a major part of their own golf history. What Bill and others began to realize was that history is no longer the important ingredient it once was to players of note. Today, it is all about the money and convenience. It would have been fun to have past winners but unfortunately, no one was prepared to put the kind of monies they were asking for into the evening's budget. Show business, indeed!

In stark comparison to today's demands, Claude Harmon's past assistants came back to the Club in 1988 for three days of honoring Claude's long-time bag room manager, "Moe" Delaporte. At least 30 very well-known professionals took the time to be part of Winged Foot's – and their own – history. The sense of "family" expressed by the participants over the three days was palpable and genuine.

That money continues to be the operative factor in today's tournament world can be seen in teaching rates to all comers. Even if you could get a date with a David Leadbetter, or even a Sean Foley, plan to spend thousands of dollars, not the hundreds of yesteryear. The irony is that all you really have to do is sit in front of your television on almost any weekday, and for the price of your cable bill, you can get two hours worth of lessons from most anybody, even a Leadbetter or Jim McLean once in a while.

And, here's something else to consider. Claude Harmon once said when asked about taking lessons, "I wouldn't take a lesson from someone that can't break eighty in a tournament." Most of today's teachers are well qualified for the task at hand, but you can't say that Claude didn't warn you!

Finally, we are now at the point where the names of the tournaments no longer reflect the site of the event. The Western Open or Los Angeles Open or whatever, is now recognized by the name of the sponsor, i.e., Mercedes or American Express, or AT&T. Fortunately, charity also benefits from this sponsorship activity, but all of the speeches and awards are most often given in the name of the sponsor.

There is now no question that golf has taken its place on the American television stage as major entertainment. Indeed, when one watches today's coverage of the major championships, they have become large enough to take their places right along with the Kentucky Derby, the Super Bowl or the World Series.

One thing we now know is happening to the game is that the tournament courses are getting more difficult to play and the expense is mounting with every tournament held. It could also be that heavy television coverage of major events is simply encouraging people to think that the game is in such excellent shape that we need to do very little to insure its safe passage to a questionable future. Still, there now seems to be a pervasive lack of interest in golf stars that are simply "ordinary."

Tiger's nearly year-long absence from the TOUR and now the entrance of younger stars into the game makes the point that televised interest peaks only when there is a superstar involved. The question of whether sponsors are going to continue to fund televised golf without a legitimate star is clearly up for an answer – and the answer may not be to a network's advantage. Or the game's.

EVERYBODY SHOULD HAVE A GOLF PUBLICATION

CHAPTER 7

BEL-AIR CC., BEVERLY HILLS, CALIFORNIA, JUNE, 1985

You get to see movie and television stars here. Tom Snyder, a fellow Winged Foot member and long-time talk show host, invited me to play Bel-Air Country Club when I was in Los Angeles for a GOLF Magazine/Times Mirror meeting. Bel-Air's men's locker room is a very dark area and it is difficult to make out who is coming at you even when they are no more than 20 feet away. Tom spoke across the room to a shadowy figure saying that "he'd like to introduce him to a friend of his from New York."

Out of the gloom came the instantly recognizable face of Bob Newhart. I couldn't have been more impressed or surprised to meet the famous man. My surprise lasted only a few seconds when Snyder said, "Arnold is the publisher of GOLF Magazine. He has dozens of readers!" At the time, the magazine's circulation was just over 1 million subscribers – somewhat higher than a dozen.

Newhart's irrepressible and dry response was right out of his television show: "Very nice to meet you. I'm glad things are going so smoothly for you at GOLF Magazine!"

Despite the star power, the men's grillroom conversations were absolutely the same at every other club in the world. Jokes were being told, someone wanted a favor from a studio head and someone else had just gotten off the Nationwide Tour. West Coast golf was pretty much on track.

~~~~~~~~~~~~~~~~~~~~~~~~

In the early 1980s, I moved from *TIME* Magazine in the Time-Life Building on 6th Avenue to Madison Avenue as publisher of *GOLF* Magazine. I thought that at this stage in my life, I would get to play a little more golf but instead I ended up in the same meetings that I had just left. Times Mirror, out of Los Angeles, owned the New York City-based publishing unit and while they certainly understood newspapers, there didn't seem to be as much understanding as to how to promote a magazine, never mind a golf publication.

I should have known I was probably in the wrong place when, after a week at the new company, I was asked by a man that I had just met to "stop by his office."

The next day I went to his office. He closed his door and told me, "he was going to fire the man that just hired me." The man speaking to me was Jack Scott, the president of the Magazine Division of Times Mirror.

A week later, Herb Schnall, the chairman of the company asked me to, "Stop by his office." I had never met him but at least he didn't shut his door when he told me, "The man who fired the man who hired you will be leaving the company shortly."

As this did not sound like a promising start – or a very good career move – I did the only logical thing: I went down in the elevator and got a drink in the bar across the street.

When it came to golf, neither *Golf Digest* nor *GOLF* Magazine strayed very far from the instructional formula that had become traditional – and successful – in the men's market. Both magazines were monthlies with circulations of just over one million copies each. Very little editorial emphasis was given to either the emerging female market or the coming retirement market.

It wasn't until American Express started its *Travel and Leisure* and Meredith Corporation started *Golf for Women* that the female market was given its just due. *Golf for Women* went eventually with Condé Nast, the same stable which purchased the *Golf Digest* publications, but despite its editorial excellence, it is unfortunately now out of business. In what is a personal irony, I never really had to leave the Time-Life Building at all because within a few years, Time Inc. brought *GOLF* Magazine into the fold, buying the entire Magazine Group from Times Mirror!

In 1988, I became involved with a new publication out of Hilton Head, South Carolina called *Southern Links*. Jack Purcell Sr., the former Executive Vice-President of CBS, bought the publication from a gentleman by the name of Fred Wynn. It is now simply called *Links* and is owned by Purcell's son, also Jack, who bought it from his father.

The early roots of *Southern Links*, started by a Hilton Head resident named Mark Brown, came about through a finely-tuned marketing analysis that took place in a Hilton Head saloon. Brown, who would go on to design golf courses, had just sold his interest in a Hilton Head Island real estate/golf publication and had run an ad in a local paper asking for investors to put up $10,000 each to start a new golf magazine. Fred Wynn, who had just retired from his family business, Burrell's Clipping Service, in New Jersey, answered the ad.

According to island lore, the "marketing analysis", apparently went something like this: "Nice to meet you Mark, what are you gong to do now?"

Brown replied that "He had no idea. Maybe a similar publication regionally in the entire South."

"Like the idea," said Wynn. "How much money do you need?"

Brown figured $100,000 would be the right number. Wynn said, " Fine, I'll take 50% of the company as an investment and you take 50% to run it."

Two months later, Brown called Wynn and mentioned that he needed another $100,000.

Wynn asked, "Why?"

Brown said, "Next issue." Enter the Purcells.

The publication is now in its 24th year.

Another equally good idea that had strong advertising potential was a publication out of Boston called *Senior Golfer*. It was started in the early 1990s by a publishing group that correctly decided that since seniors play half the rounds of golf in the country, that a publication devoted to their golf-related life style might work.

And it did work for a while, particularly when their editors concentrated on regional real estate with reviews of the golf courses and clubs within the region being featured. After all, the retirement market was starting to look hot and certain upscale advertisers were quickly becoming aware of the baby boomer market.

What *Senior Golfer* really had as its domain was a powerful merchandising vehicle that could promote all sorts of extremely valuable retirement activities and products. That would include brokers, mutual funds, investment houses, insurance, real estate, cameras, lawn equipment, expensive cars, homes and home refurbishment. That market has turned out to be the largest market of them all.

Alas, the magazine got wobbly when its editors decided, with approval from management, that it would become a golf instruction magazine rather than a promotion vehicle. The problem was that hitting a shot out of sand is exactly the same for an 11-year old as it is as for a 61-year old. And there were already dozens of magazines that told people of all ages how to hit out of sand or for that matter any other golf shot that people needed to know. The magazine finally folded.

Some observers said that the word *Senior* in the title, itself, made readers uneasy and unwilling to admit that they qualified for the senior ranks. Today, however, the word is far more acceptable as an entire generation moves into senior status. In fact, most of the products now advertised in the golf world are senior-oriented.

One of the latest wrinkles in the industry is a growing number of companies that are entering the sports marketing field. Time Warner's Turner Sports Interactive operates Web sites for various sports organizations, including the PGA of America that was about to put up a site with tee time availability and travel information as this is being written. Management stated that the site will primarily bring sports event highlights to an audience that "doesn't have time to watch the event all the way through and doesn't want to be left out of the conversation."

And, a few years ago out of Philadelphia came the news that the Wharton School has just entered the world of sport with the "Wharton Sports Business Initiative." The announcement outlined that "the new center will position Wharton as a premier player in the sports business industry." The release went on to say that "WSBI will serve as a nucleus for all sports business related activities at Wharton. Further, it will include a speaker series that will "be aimed at conferences and forums." One of the most recent entries into the field is now coming from, of all places, Manhattanville College in Purchase, New York.

As various corporations and schools build complete departments devoted to sports, golf remains somewhat of a conundrum to most professional publishers and television producers. Except for the majors, they tend to shy away from golf simply because they've learned the hard way that the sport doesn't automatically support a high-volume advertising marketplace.

The New York City area is typical of most big golf markets in the U.S. The Metropolitan Golf Association has it own monthly publication, *The Met Golfer*, which goes to virtually all of the various member clubs and their members in the area. Like other local golf publications, it has been in the hands of several publishers over the years. *Executive Golfer* is circulated through "bench" distribution in locker rooms. Additionally, there are other regional publications covering real estate, public courses, hotels and local restaurants. Unfortunately, few of these publications are large enough to attract anything but limited advertising dollars.

From time to time, someone is always trying to dominate the market or make a purchase of one of the larger golf publications. Some 35 years ago, Lillian Harlow and her son, Dick, who then owned *Golf World* out of Pinehurst North Carolina, decided to sell the weekly publication to any and all comers. I found myself bidding on the property along with John deGarmo, still the president of his own ad agency. Unfortunately, we soon found out that another bidder had surfaced.

It turned out that the bidder was a man named John McCarthy, who was also a member at Winged Foot. Had we known that, we could have moved further down the bar and made a threesome out of our bid. Instead, the property was ultimately bought by Crain Communications out of Chicago. A footnote is warranted here: The original John McCarthy was not related to the current John McCarthy, a later and well-known member of Winged Foot.

I am occasionally asked the difference between *Golf Digest* and *GOLF* Magazine since they are so similar in monthly circulation size, I've shortened the answer to that question by reciting an incident that occurred when Jay Fitzgerald was publisher of *Golf Digest* and I held the same position at *GOLF* Magazine. Some loose cannon, and still unknown, executive pointed out to the management of both corporations that since Jay and I were members of the same golf club, that it would be logical to assume that we were "colluding" on the advertising rates for each publication. Nothing could be further from the truth and I even had to look up the meaning of the word in the dictionary.

The problem became pronounced when the two of us, plus staff members, were scheduled on the same airplane headed for the January PGA Merchandising Show in Orlando, Florida. The plane did not depart on time due to winter weather conditions and both staffs sat apart in the lounge for several hours.

We did not speak.

Finally, both groups decided to have a drink with each other and play some "team" gin rummy. Both activities continued even as the plane was finally in mid-air and well on its way to Florida. It occurred to both of us that we were treading on thin ice. Nevertheless, you should know that we never heard the word "collusion" ever again.

Being involved with so many publications has kept me in touch with all sorts of golfers and venues that have produced many acquaintances and even long-term friends. Some were big names, others not so well-known. Some are still in business and others are gone. Nevertheless, they all centered on something that nearly everyone can agree is pure fun and well-worth the time and effort.

I know I would do it all over again.

Indeed, everybody should have a golf publication!

CULTURE SHIFT

CHAPTER 8

LA QUINTA COUNTRY CLUB, PALM SPRINGS, CALIFORNIA, 1967

Tom Nieporte, the long-time professional at Winged Foot, won the Bob Hope Classic in 1967. On his way to the tournament he had an early morning departure from his Florida home. In the morning darkness, Tom picked a pair of shoes out of his closet that were similar but not matching. He could do nothing after arriving in Palm Springs but use the shoes.

At the award presentation, following his victory, President and Mrs. Eisenhower were in attendance along with Mr. Hope. Mrs. Eisenhower sat next to Tom for the ceremonies. At some point in the festivities Mrs. Eisenhower happened to look down and spotted Tom's non-matching shoes.

"Tom, do you realize you have shoes on that don't match?" asked Mrs. Eisenhower.

"Absolutely, Mrs. Eisenhower," replied Tom. "Would you believe that I have a pair at home just like them?"

～～～～～～～～～～～

The stark fact is that women have now changed the face of golf forever.

Dick Ryan, the noted lawyer from Ryan and Stanton in New

York, and long-time legal advisor to the golf industry observed that "The advance of women toward memberships can probably be directly traced back to World War II when women took over many male jobs while the men were overseas. Certainly the advent of the double income family in the '80's has sped up the changing face of American golf," said Ryan.

Most golf observers agree that the single-income husband of yesteryear had to make a major decision about his marriage. He could continue to go play golf with the boys or he could get a divorce.

Indeed, there was a time shortly after World War II, particularly in the Midwest, when Mom, Dad and the kids all went to the country club for lunch on Saturdays and Sundays. After lunch, the kids went to the pool and Mom would go to the tennis court or play bridge. Dad hit the links, of course. On occasion, Dad would be joined by one of the male offspring for an extra nine holes. On rare occasions it would be a daughter.

Today, a startling number of women are now starting to hit the cover off the ball. It's very disconcerting to be in your Sunday mixed foursome with a woman that is 5'-4" and 135 pounds and is hitting the ball 250 yards and straight. Out on the LPGA Tour, Michelle Wie was 15-years old and hitting it 300 yards. The only thing that saves the day for male egos is that on the PGA TOUR, they are now hitting it upwards of 380 yards at times.

And, whether dad wants to admit it or not, women are very often more fun to play with than some serious grouch. A considerable number of them are combining golf and business as successfully as their male counterparts.

What was once clearly a male domain has been shifted to what is now being called "Gender Neutral" – a term that no one ever thought they would be dealing with. For those clubs that wish to retain a relationship with outside tournament activities, the term is now written into the by-laws.

However, some rough patches are popping up along the way. The most visible controversy has been Martha Burk's argument with Augusta National concerning admitting a female member. Hootie Johnson, then Augusta's Chairman, was asked what he would do if Martha showed up the Masters. He told *The New York Times* that he would "take her on a tour of the course in his cart and would treat her with all proper Augusta hospitality."

Ms. Burk's response to the entire situation was one of total disdain for the event and the club. As was noted also in *The New York Times*: "Her organization condemns all companies that participate in these clubs."

"This is not only an outrage for taxpayers, it is an insult to stockholders and female employees," Ms. Burk argued.

Two Democratic House members, Carolyn Maloney of New York and Brad Sherman of California, announced at the same time that they were planning to introduce legislation that would "cut off tax breaks for businesses using clubs that discriminated."

What appears to have happened in the Augusta situation is that two distinctly different issues were, without intent, combined. The first issue is whether the legal and political system can force – or at the very least, coerce – the admission of women into a men's-only club. The second issue is how far an outside agency can go in making it difficult for a sponsor to promote their products on a televised event broadcast from an all male club.

There seems to be an assumption in the press, that a club for "males only" must somehow be a club that is simultaneously "against females." To that point, Representative Maloney was quoted in a *Times* story: "Augusta has a tradition of discrimination."

There is now even the question of who will play on what Tour regardless of venue. The announcement came several years ago that the previously all-male British Open will welcome females to its field. R&A Secretary Peter Dawson commented on the new eligibility: "There has been no resistance to the principle of women playing golf in the British Open if they are qualified for it." The U.S. Open has never had a rule against women trying to qualify for the championship.

In a call to the LPGA to see if a reverse request had come in from male professionals, a spokeswoman for the organization stated that when it comes to a man playing on the LPGA Tour, the LPGA "has a clause that restricts the tour to females (at birth)." The LPGA spokeswoman continued, "If they were ever to be faced with a serious discrimination case, it would fall into the category of a 'Public Policy Exception." That caveat presumably gets them around so-called "discrimination" problems.

The obvious handicap, at the moment, for women competing against men is pure strength: i.e., how far they can hit the ball. However, the minute a significant number of women begin hitting the ball as far as men, the legal ambulance chasers will be out in force on both sides of the argument. The only two come immediately to mind who really could hit the ball a really long way are Babe Zaharias and JoAnne Carner. And it's worth noting that Michelle Wie did try unsuccessfully to qualify for the U.S. Open.

At the moment, the only current course of action for an all-male club, short of changing to "gender neutral," is to drop out of commercial tournaments and corporate activity altogether. "Once you start to attract outside sponsors and you want to run an international tournament, that changes the rules regarding rights of association," observes Donna Shalala, the former Secretary of Health and Human Services in the Clinton administration and current President of the University of Miami.

There's more. The simple act of getting into or even staying in a "gender neutral" club can still be very tricky for women. If a divorcee remarries, the membership committee will want to take a look at the new husband with the very real possibility of turning him down. Widows can usually keep a membership, but remarrying could end that as well.

With the current downturn in core rounds of golf being played annually, there has been a move to attract more women to the game. One of the major problems is the number of young women who go on to other sports, leaving golf adrift in their own lives. They leave it to the young men who seem more likely to stay with the game through adulthood.

Still, there are some things involving women's golf that will forever remain the same. It is absolutely clear, for example, that if a fairway is too far for most women to reach, the Women's Golf Committee in clubs across the country will politely ask their Green's Committee one more time to move up the red markers – surely not an unreasonable request.

At this same time, the prizes for women's tournaments might be decided. Some of us will get new birdhouses for our porches, while others will have brightly colored salad forks in the kitchen. My favorite is the pewter salt and pepper shaker set with the club logo done in light blue cork.

LAWYERS ARE HERE ALSO

CHAPTER 9

OLD WARSON COUNTRY CLUB, ST. LOUIS, MISSOURI, AUGUST, 1958

*K*yle Rote who, at the time, was still in his New York Giant days, took part in the early stable of promotional athletes put together by Sports Illustrated. On this occasion, Kyle was assigned to promotional duty for the magazine in St. Louis. On an off-afternoon, we were invited to play Old Warson with Dutch Harrison, the club professional and former PGA TOUR regular.

Old Warson was also the home club for Charles Lindbergh. After golf, the SI group was taken to the "Lindbergh" room in the clubhouse, where the great man's post-flight photo was supposed to be hanging. It was not hanging. Apparently Lindbergh had made some pro-Nazi political comments in the late 1930s and early '40s that the membership did not like. His photo was laid against the wall, on the floor, backwards. It sat there, untouched, for several years.

To my knowledge, the photo could still be on the floor. No one in our group made a comment, but Rote did point out that even by the most severe political standards, that's a tough penalty. Looking back, we all concluded that it could also be one of the first ventures of a political nature to visit the golf club scene in the United States.

At almost warp speed, complex social issues are coming at clubs and golf as a whole with increasing frequency. What seemed like simple decisions to be made by a club in the past, i.e., whether to put a new watering system in or whether to replace the sand in the traps, are rapidly being replaced by far more complicated social decisions.

Cocktail parties at the club are still just as much fun, but there are now designated drivers, a vast improvement over some of those dicey drives home of yesteryear. While the club luncheon is still visited by an occasional cocktail, there is no question that the venerable advertising gatherings portrayed recently in TV's "Mad Men" are gone forever. And with them went some very amazing happenings.

That would include *TIME* Magazine's Eddie Stewart and Bob Gardanier, both outstanding sales executives in the 1950s and '60s. Stewart and Gardanier had just played in a golf outing at Greenwich (CT) Country Club and stayed for dinner. Following dinner, the procedure was to drive Gardanier home with Stewart continuing on to his home. It was also a time when the State of Connecticut was taking away drivers' licenses "for life" if a serious infraction occurred.

Unknown to both golfers, the Greenwich police had been alerted to an armed robbery of a gas station in town and they were looking for a red Chevrolet. Gardanier and Stewart were driving a red Chevrolet and on the winding Greenwich back roads, the police pulled them over.

The first officer asked the two to step out of the car. In their business suits, they stood beside each other in the glare of the police lights. Coming down the far side of the road was a second officer, with his hand on his belt.

The first officer asked, "Gentlemen, may I see some identification?"

"Certainly, officer," said Stewart, reaching into his inside breast pocket to pull out the proper documentation.

The second Greenwich officer, walking the side of the road, reacted instantly to Stewart's hand going toward his pocket, by aiming his pistol at both red Chevrolet "criminals." Gardanier, immediately stuck his fingers in his ears, anticipating the loud report the officer's gun was about to make. It was a scene right out of a Marx Brothers movie!

Both Greenwich policemen gave a resigned wave of the hand to the "criminals," got back in the patrol car and drove off looking for the real red Chevrolet. One can only imagine the conversation back in police barracks later that evening about the case of the "Great Gasoline Station Robbery."

There has obviously been a major shift in both club and business lifestyles over the past 25 years. But, while those days have faded, it is now also true that more and more equally sticky social questions are now being taken from the golf club directly to court.

In the early 80's, a major lawsuit was won by a group of women from Haverhill Country Club outside of Boston. Finding themselves in a hostile male environment that included no lockers, no grillroom and tee times that were inconvenient and discriminatory, these women were among the first to be successful in court. Several million dollars were awarded in the case and lawyers across the country began their ritual dance. Nevertheless, the warning bell was sounded and the words "gender neutral" have been officially written into the by-laws of most clubs in the nation.

There are now lawsuits that seriously question the ability of a club to turn down applicants when a significant number of members would like to have the candidate in the club. On the other side of the coin, there currently has been at least one legal action where those members who wrote letters of disapproval were themselves in the process of being sued for defamation of character.

Clubs that have not been paying attention to their property boundaries abutting their course also find themselves in court under a law called "Adverse Possession." Quietly, neighbors who have been caring for an adjacent parcel belonging to the club can actually claim the land as their own under that law after a period of seven years. Several large metropolitan clubs have already lost a corner or an adjacent piece of land to vigilant neighbors.

Lately, homes along the fairways are now taking a page out of the liability files, by suing the neighboring club for threatening the safety of their dwelling and its occupants. Again, many clubs across the country are now in courtrooms defending themselves against home-owning neighbors who claim that they have been hit by an aggressive slice or two. What usually solves the problem is for the club to buy the property in question and keep it for eventual club use or re-write the bill of sale to prevent a new owner from taking similar legal action.

Further, entire towns are starting to fight back hard when a developer attempts to put a new golf course in. Conversely, if the development can add substantially to the town's tax base, they can fight equally hard to get the project completed despite the strenuous objections of local environmentalists.

Builders have gotten somewhat smarter about constructing new homes on a new golf course. There was a time when the best land on a new project was used for home sites. The golf course was then shoe-horned in on less desirable land with result that the course was often not an inviting layout. Developers are reversing this procedure, with homes on the more difficult acreage and a superior layout on the best land.

Then there is the question of club management itself. The day of selecting governing club officials on the basis of their professional job capabilities is now rapidly disappearing. Instead, many clubs have resorted to a crony system and the results are often less than spectacular.

Here's a conversation worth recording: "I've been asked to go on the board. What's it like?"

"First, you have to check your brains at the door," replies the current board member.

"What do you do at the meetings?" asks the candidate.

"You change everything the previous board put in," replies the board member.

"Is that all there is to it?

"Yes, it's very complicated."

A number of older clubs have gone a long way toward solving the problem of rapidly changing boards through a two-tier system of management. The first level, consisting of a permanent board of governors, is made up of senior members of the club. They often sit on that board for extended periods of time, some for life.

The second level of management is an executive director level that serves shorter terms and handles the month-by-month details of the club – along with the club manager and head golf professional. In this way, the temptation to "put one's stamp" on club direction is counter-balanced by the long-term direction of the permanent board. And most often, long-term's primary management function has to do with major improvements and concurrent costs, tournament approvals, and complicated legal issues.

Much of today's club direction is coming from better ball-strikers who, by definition, don't share the same thinking as to what the bulk of their 20-handicap membership would like to have done, or not done, to the golf course. Lower handicap players and course developers usually do not produce forgiving golf courses. What's more discouraging, 20-handicappers rarely say a word about these decisions.

In another direction, same-sex marriages or registered domestic partners are right now in various legal actions forcing clubs to provide the same membership rights bestowed on male-female marriages. It is reported that a major club in the Atlanta area was in litigation, testing whether same sex married couples can be excluded from club membership. The city apparently won its lawsuit against discrimination but now the state has since ruled against the city.

Even the discipline of a member has taken on a legal tone that can get the club in trouble if it is not handled in accordance to the letter of the law.

The 2002 Sarbanes-Oxley Act, which was aimed at "for profit" improprieties in our public corporations, has now empowered a number of elected officials to insist many of those regulations apply to tax-exempt social clubs as well. On the other hand, James Reilly in an article in the "CPA Journal" points out that the applicability of the Act does not, in fact, extend to social clubs.

Few issues are easy these days.

Further complicating the legal landscape are questions of immigration procedures as they relate to club employment. Many employees are coming from immigrant ranks and there is now pressure from various states to limit many of these temporary workers. In an opposing direction, The National Club Association in Washington, D.C. indicates that there is actually a shortage of clubhouse and maintenance workers, and there is a legitimate need to attract legal immigration.

One of the more challenging of all golf club issues could very well be that many communities are increasingly running out of funds and the potential exists for property evaluation procedures to substantially increase property taxes on various local private golf clubs. In fact, most clubs are already aware of the danger and have lobbied for laws that allow a club to retain a minimum property tax structure.

According to Larry Hirsh, President of Golf Property Analysts in

Conshohocken, Pennsylvania, many club property taxes in various states are based on a system that considers the "highest and best use of a structure or a piece of land." While this is an increasingly common basis for evaluation, many other states have property tax laws that can be based on price per acre or a cash-flow multiple. Other clubs, under different rules, can be taxed as "undeveloped land" or "farmland." Some states assess golf clubs as "operating clubs" which often results in lower values than may be realized from an alternative use. Certain other clubs can protect a favorably-assessed value by donating that land to the state or the community through an "open space conservation easement."

The National Golf Foundation now pegs the number of private clubs vs. public fee courses as being in a dramatic switch. Since 1990, the number of public courses has increased from 8,036 to 11,628 with almost all of this increase in the high-end sector and at 18 holes. Private clubs have not kept pace by dropping from 4,810 to 4,262. However, the major portion of this decline came in the nine hole course category.

The possible steady increase in public courses, even given the number that eventually switch to private in order to make ends meet, could point to the ultimate direction of the game if it is to expand. If the slow-play problem can be answered at America's public courses, we could be well on the way to resembling the European or "British Isles" golf course model.

At the same time, resort courses are increasing in numbers. They are rapidly expanding the whole concept of taking a golfing vacation, satisfying the desire to play for an extended period of time without plunking down large amounts of initiation monies.

It could very well be that the term for most private clubs will be replaced with the more accurate "country" clubs. These will be many miles away in less crowded countryside areas. In a hundred years or so, we'll put the whole family in the car for the day or a weekend just for golf. We also may be driving to Vermont from New York City or somewhere equally distant. Or it could be Pittsburgh to West Virginia. Business golf will have to figure that one out, since it's hard to get to Vermont and back to New York City in one day. Maybe a commercial F27 will make a comeback!

Unless you've already moved your office to Vermont.

THE FUTURE

CHAPTER 10

OAKMONT COUNTRY CLUB, PITTSBURGH, PENNSYLVANIA, JUNE, 1953

I watched my first U.S. Open with my dad at Oakmont, outside of Pittsburgh, in 1953. That year Ben Hogan won. I saw my second at Winged Foot in 1959 after I had joined the sales staff of Sports Illustrated. Bill Casper won with marvelous putting. The club and the USGA allowed SI to have the now famous entertainment tent that stood alone at the edge of the 15th green.

Today, tents are the order of the day, with corporation after corporation lined up in a row. We've come all the way from walking the fairways with the contestants to joining one more cocktail party in an elaborate tent. Televised golf is turning into a sport by itself; witness the growth in audience size when a major star is in the hunt. Amateur play is running out of public enthusiasm. Fairways are longer. Finally, we are watching older venues being eliminated for championship consideration because of a lack of space for parking and tents.

Some of this can be reversed, of course. Some of it need not be changed and some of it will never return to the game. However, to continue raising the amount of money now needed to play the game or join a club must be addressed, if golf is to be a sport that one and all can continue to play. Young golfers that are introduced to the game by organizations like The First Tee must have places to play that they can afford.

My guess is that today's golfers and its leaders are smart enough to know what's coming at them and they'll do the things that are now needed to put the game on a path to continue the sport's inherent value to all of us.

~~~~~~~~~~~~~~~~~~~~~~

There are those that think the entire concept of golf in America needs a new "business model."

With the exception of a weekday outing, one can walk onto most private courses during any given week and hardly find a soul playing. As a result, caddy programs are being hurt, as are the dining rooms and club exchequers. Certain well-known metropolitan clubs are fortunate to have rather solid waiting lists of people eager to join the club even with initiation fees in the hundreds of thousands of dollars. This, however, is not the typical case.

There are now many more private and semi-private clubs, even public courses, now looking for members or customers and will be digging deeper when the current recession ends. Further, a significant number of developers who built public courses are now reconfiguring their operations to go private in the hopes that financing will be better in the private sector. Many private clubs are starting to charge lesser guest fees to help encourage more play and club use by members who are reluctant to pay the prohibitively high guest and caddy fees now involved.

There are now a number of state golf association executives that are starting to question why many new golf courses are so user "unfriendly." Too often, Mr. and Mrs. Newly Retired are often dismayed and discouraged by courses that are, even by top amateur standards, too long and too tough. They are equally reluctant to purchase homes on such a course, which defeats the whole idea of a developer trying to get someone to join a far-away club for a second home site.

Until the recent economic meltdown, far too many golf courses were spending enormous sums of money on "improvements" that were putting a future financial strain on these same clubs. The theory is that it is cheaper to fix something "now" rather than in the future. It is still money that probably shouldn't have been expended.

Multi-million dollar watering systems have been put in place by many clubs, where older, less-sophisticated systems worked just fine. Expensive sand traps have been added 75 yards down a fairway at 280 yards out, to suit absolutely nobody except a few touring professionals or top amateurs. Trees are cut down with little thought as to why they were put up in the first place. Usually the original reason was to protect a player from an errant shot launched from an adjacent fairway.

Elaborate clubhouse renovations are taking place with corresponding assessments being handed out to the members. Two, in Connecticut, a few years back sent out assessments to each member in the $35,000 range. The original clubhouses were just fine. In defense of one of the new Connecticut clubhouses, one young investment banker said that the current clubhouse was "antiquated." Tell that to the members of the R&A at St.Andrews!

One can "join" Carnoustie for a modest sum if one lives in the town. St. Andrews has an annual fee for a resident that was, and still may be the equivalent of $400. Granted, many of these courses get considerable revenue from overseas visitors, but even those fees are unfortunately starting to creep upwards. Still, the simple answer over the years is that their business model has been that many of the British Isles courses and clubhouses do not require the enormous capital investments that their U.S. counterparts seem to need.

There is a strong case to be made, by those closest to the game, that ex-players turned architects and developers are, in themselves, counter-productive. Where drainage and clubhouse problems were once solved by very competent club members that had equal, or even better, expertise in whatever problem had to be solved, a whole new business has grown up to take the problem away from the membership. The result is that course developers are now adding their own business expenses and staff salaries to an already rising club annual budget.

A few years ago, *The New York Times* detailed a fight over a proposed golf course between a well-to-do developer and long-time residents in Norfolk, Connecticut. The course planned to charge a $150,000 initiation fee. Roland Betts, the developer and college fraternity brother of former President George W. Bush, was quoted as saying the course is for friends that "have money and like to golf."

There it is again. Bring money.

Here was a chance for an entire community, whether one played golf or not, to participate in a discussion of an asset that will be in the community for a long period of time. In fact, quoting *The Times*, at the time when the Norfolk course was being considered, one of the main critics of the project, one Wheaton Byers, suggested an alternative nine-hole course further down the mountain from the planned project.

This brings up the entire question of "eminent domain" which may, sooner rather than later, become a major part of golf's dialogue. Town after town are now running out of public lands and golf courses often represent the last vestige of "in-town" land. Deepdale Golf Club on Long Island has already come under fire a few years ago, by a mayor that saw an opportunity to turn the club into a village-owned golf facility. Deepdale won that skirmish, but the thought has been permanently planted in golf's psyche that any given town or village could keep the original facility as a golf course, but it would no longer be private. And, more often than not, the town can simply wait until the club runs short of members or cash, whichever comes first.

The future of golf could very well be a network of public and municipal courses where the ebb and flow of regional public play is shared through control and funding by various developers and the counties themselves. In a very real sense, the course could end up being modeled after the simple courses so prevalent in this country in the mid '40s when the game started its widespread expansion.

Left to our own devices, we have too often built what could be called the crushing "U.S." model that has led to needlessly high expenditures as the years wear on. Less-complicated structures and courses can lead back to better expenditure levels and proper time requirements for the nation's golfing families.

The fact is, that under current circumstances, public golf still takes too long. Five-hour rounds are the norm. At Putnam National, a public course in Putnam County, New York, an interview with their then-general manager pointed out that the private club player has been "schooled" properly: i.e. plays the game at a level that is generally faster than the public course player. Certainly, there are excellent players on public courses, but just a few beginners can slow the whole day down.

He further pointed out that since the public is putting down hard cash for a starting time that apparently and automatically allows the fee player to defend his style of play, slow or otherwise. Fortunately, the private club has far more control over slow play. If public courses are to continue a pattern of growth in comparison to a private club, faster play will be a key factor.

Several clubs have suggested that its entire membership go through an annual breakfast concerning slow play. Who has heard lately about any board, anywhere, sending a slow-play warning letter to anyone in its membership?

Still, there have been some fascinating events centering on slow play. In his first year at Tedesco, Tony Fletcher, a long-time friend and golfing partner, simply walked up to the slow group ahead and somehow wound up in a fist fight (which he won). Several members felt he should be immediately suspended, but one veteran of club politics suggested that Fletcher should be considered as the next president of the club.

On the other hand, some players occasionally go so fast that they crowd the group in front, even though that group is playing at proper speed. A foursome from Woodland Golf Club in Newton, Massachusetts, was playing a winter round in Florida when they began to notice a husband and wife coming up behind them. After several holes the twosome became increasingly impatient. Both groups began to argue – an argument which was settled when the couple's very expensive poodle spotted a nearby alligator. The poodle charged and the alligator did what alligators do. We do know at this writing if the couple ever recovered from their loss. No further words were exchanged.

A word here about carts: In many clubs, they have completely taken over and caddies have disappeared. To that point, a story surfaced about the late Mike Souchak, the PGA TOUR's leading money winner in 1955 and one-time head professional at Oakland Hills. When Mike took over as Director of Golf at Innisbrook outside Tampa some 25 years ago, he apparently signed a contract with Innisbrook management that took a small dollar amount for each of several hundred carts going out each day. Everybody was happy – that is until management did the math and figured out how much Mike was collecting each day from the hundreds of carts going out. They obviously asked Mike to re-do the contract since he was probably making more money than anyone else associated with Innisbrook.

Still, there are a great number of clubs that have figured out how to have both caddies and carts in tandem. Several clubs in the New York area allow carts on the course after 3 p.m. Should a foursome go out in two carts, a single fore-caddy is sent out with the group. The fees are $50.00 for each cart and $35.00 per bag per player. With two people splitting a cart and one caddy raking the traps and tending the pin for the entire foursome, the total cost is $60.00 per man with $100.00 going to the club and $140.00 going to the caddy!

In yet another direction, certain major clubs are changing their thinking about holding large tournaments every 15 years or so. The Country Club in Brookline, Massachusetts, has made the decision to forego large gallery events in their future. The 1999 Ryder Cup at Brookline had 45,000 people in daily attendance and according to one observer there was simply not enough room for the event. To get a look at the matches, one had to pick a spot and stay there. Going to another location was out of the question. Plus, the bar was open.

Based on that experience, The Country Club decided not to hold the PGA Championship scheduled at that club in 2005. Instead, it was switched to Baltusrol in New Jersey. At the same time, Brookline has elected not to have the U.S. Open in 2013 that would have celebrated the 100th Anniversary of Francis Ouimet's world-renown victory in 1913.

It is possible that Brookline will, in the future, host some smaller tournaments such as the Walker Cup or the U.S. Amateur but, in all likelihood, the day of the major event is over at Brookline. Winged Foot, in 2009, turned down the 2015 U.S. Open, feeling that it was too close to the last Open held at the club in 2006.

Not only are the older venues no longer large enough for both corporate tents and parking, there is an increasing question as to how much time and revenue is needed to get them in shape for the tournament, and then repair the course following the event. Several officials have already pointed out what could happen if members from nearby clubs no longer provided marshalling or administration assistance on a voluntary basis.

It is entirely possible that future events will increasingly be played on public venues such as Whistling Straits or Bethpage Black. Many private club members are beginning to breathe a sigh of relief at the thought that there will be no more majors to contend with at their club.

And, wait until you hear the argument about standardizing the ball. It is undergoing tests right now by the USGA and golf could very soon take its place with other sports with an official ball. The fact that the USGA and the PGA have, until recently, been quiet while manufacturers have constantly refined and improved equipment that have forced clubs to put tremendous expense into lengthening their courses is more than disconcerting.

Should the ball be standardized? My guess is that sports fans or even on-air announcers won't like the idea of a Tiger Woods or Rory McIlroy hitting the ball only 245 or even 275 yards with everybody virtually dead even in their distances. The public is now used to seeing everything not tied down being hit over the fence. At Baltusrol's 17th hole at the 2005 PGA, the tee was set so far back it required a drive of at least 270 yards just to get to the fairway.

John Daly can shoot his 77's and 78's, but he often draws the second-largest TOUR galleries. No one cares what John shoots. He just has to pound the ball to the moon. Corporate television sponsorship would flag among advertisers that wish to convey power or strength should the ball be standardized.

With an "official" ball rule, you can have very interesting first tee conversations.

Isn't that the new Titleist "Grasshopper?" "I heard it's designed for Open courses."

"Yeah," It hops onto the fairway as soon as it's hit into the rough."

Looking ahead, a number of golf officials have brought up, once again, the entire question of championship amateur play and where it will fit in an age of televised professional golf. Disappearing fast are the many long-standing amateur championships that used to be a factor as to who went on to be a professional player. There was a time when Billy Joe Patton could stay in the lumber business in North Carolina, and even Francis Ouimet, himself, could stay a world re-known amateur while pursuing business in other fields. Ditto for Bobby Jones.

Today, young players are coming out of college, going directly to the professional ranks with barely a season of amateur competition at their own state level. A shocking number of them never come close to making it, and are left to pick up the pieces of a career by teaching or working their way up the club professional ladder.

Meanwhile, most of their age group competitors are going on to graduate school and into a career that very often pays much better than golf. There have been estimates that the number of amateurs and young professionals trying to catch the brass ring is now some 15,000 strong, many playing on golf circuits that have names like the Hooter's Tour, or Nationwide Tour.

At the moment, several associations are already working closely with area schools and with members of their golf teams. Rather than letting these neophyte golfers simply wander into golf's future, clubs could give closer membership consideration to those that played their high school or college matches at that club.

Obviously, they would go through an admissions procedure, but keeping these young golfers in the loop could eliminate the customary 20-year hiatus of joining a club only after they have attained a major financial footing. To disregard such a pool of talented players and their friends is simply throwing away what could be a major part of a golf club's future.

Several local sportswriters have suggested that state amateur play be set up to include an expanded format of intrastate competitions, i.e., the state eastern champion could be paired against the western representative. Ditto for north and south. State-by-state competition would then culminate in going to the U.S. Amateur.

Obviously, most state champs now go on to U.S. Amateur play, but the thinking is that it could develop into a format that could build much wider state spectator and local press interest.

It might be incumbent on the state golf associations to get the attention of every newspaper, including even the large circulation publishers to include coverage of the various intrastate competitions leading to the state and national amateur championship. Today, one can hardly find the results of any local tournament in the larger area publications although several local area papers do carry area results, which is extremely important to the game.

The plain fact is that most people still pay attention to results.

Happily, the USGA put in a rule that as of January 6, 2006, the entry fees and traveling costs for a participant in various amateur tournaments can be funded by outside parties with no change in their amateur standing. If the money is supplied by a parent, no further administration is required. If it is provided by an outside agency like a club or a group of friends, the money must be sent to and recorded by the local golf association and the recipient must sign an acknowledgement of the payment.

However, even with loosening of the rules on expenses, many golf officials feel that amateur golf may never come back to the halcyon days of the early 20th century. Currently, the Metropolitan Golf Association oversees some 57 different amateur tournaments in any given year and one ex-official remarked that "no large following exists for even the most successful tournaments, except for the players themselves." Whether such a thin layer of interest is enough to sustain a high level of organized amateur competition is open to question.

There was a time on Friday afternoons in the summer, when businessmen/golfers in city after city across the country played head-to-head interclub matches. Two teams would be fielded from each club – six to eight players at scratch and six to eight players at handicap. Following 18 holes, they'd meet for cocktails and dinner.

Woodland (MA) Golf Club had, among many, a championship plaque on their grillroom wall that listed the names of three players from the 1927 team – Ted Bishop, Jess Sweetser and Francis Ouimet. All three were U.S Amateur champions, not bad for a quiet, tree-lined golf club just south of Boston! It can be admitted now that most participants played under an assumed name in case their bosses scanned the next morning's newspaper for hole-in-one notations!

As for the future of golf in business entertainment, and particularly the use of corporate jets, while those days are not totally gone, they have been severely curtailed. The pressures of IRS rulings and an economy that appeals to fewer and fewer as personal entertainment as a sales tool has, for the foreseeable future, been put on hold.

Here's a thought on that subject. Why hasn't the business community suggested that expense accounts come back at full value rather than cutting the deduction in half? Think of the jobs that would open up or better, come back under those conditions.

Many have concluded that the game is further being diminished by a "star" system, much as it has in other highly-paid entertainment venues. Our on-screen golf icons are setting our standards for enjoying the game: i.e., under-par rounds and 320-yard drives. And, when a well-known player slips a bit, the same media is quick to dissect the star's shortcomings. Given this kind of scrutiny, too many of us no longer appreciate a friend's personal best of shooting a 79, even though our friend has been trying to break 80 after over 25 years of practice and play.

Something is happening to the game and it may take several decades to sort out just exactly what is transpiring. If the golf gods want golf to make a real comeback, my guess is that the tremendous expense of today's initiation fees will have to be adjusted. Dues will similarly have to be controlled, as will daily fee structures. The increasing length in our courses will have to be reconsidered.

Indeed, the number of people that think that the game may need a new "business model" is increasing. Too many people are being forced out of the game...and we will all be the worse for it, now and for generations to come.

MULLIGAN

CHAPTER II

MENNAGIO GOLF CLUB, LAKE COMO, ITALY, 2003

*D*irectly across from the town of Bellagio, on the western side of
Lake Como, sits the town of Menaggio. The town is host to a beautiful
country course set along the side of steep mountains that lead into the
snow-capped Swiss Alps in the distance. It is breathtaking in its beauty,
and my wife and I were delighted to have the chance to play it. The
British had built the course in the 1920's and ultimately turned it over
to the Italian family that owned the adjacent farmland.

Three weeks later I was home in the United States having lunch at
Winged Foot when three gentlemen approached the table. One was Clark
Hood, a textile executive and fellow Winged Foot member, who intro-
duced two businessmen from Italy.

"Did you play golf in Italy? asked Hood.

"Did you play Menaggio? He asked.

"Yes", I said.

"Meet the owner!" exclaimed Hood.

What are the odds of meeting, three weeks later, the very man whose
family owns one of the most beautiful spots on earth? I saved this for last
because I warn you not to waste all your time on a golf course to see how
you can score. Time is too valuable for counting a score that won't mean
anything two days later anyway.

It will be the beauty and the people that will remain forever.

Sitting in my dentist's chair, I asked Mort Davidman, D.D.S. and golfer, what he thought was causing more and more people to become so intensely frustrated with their golf games. His answer could not have been more on the money.

Mort felt that, "the game is becoming too important to the people playing it."

He explained, "When people take anything seriously and they don't do well at it, they are going to be unhappy with the result."

I asked Mort if he was going to play golf on his vacation. "Absolutely not. I'm going on vacation!"

You should always ask your dentist questions about golf.

When I was first starting to play golf as a young man in the hills of Western Pennsylvania, my dad and I would go to the club and play nine holes after work on those wonderful warm, hazy, summer evenings that only Western Pennsylvania can produce. We took five clubs with us: Three, five, seven, nine-iron and putter. We'd split the clubs between the two of us, lending whatever stick was needed. You couldn't play better golf or have a better time.

The format was simple. Three-iron off the tee, with no particular expectation of hitting anywhere except "out there." In the fairway! Five-iron short of the green. Seven or nine iron near the pin. Half of the putts went in. Never hit a trap because you didn't hit it far enough to get in trouble. No caddie fees. No dragging a cart. Back to fun again. Maybe that should go before the Board!

One frustrated golfer suggested recently that golf should officially be played with only those clubs. It's a very interesting idea and one that will get you closer to "playing" the game rather than slugging the ball mindlessly.

My dad always felt that, "God randomly assigned you a lifetime handicap and he would see you back in heaven in 85 years or so."

In 1967, when I first became a member at Oakland Hills outside of Detroit, I found myself alone on the practice tee. I was soon joined by another golfer who introduced himself as Doak Walker. It was indeed, the famous football player. He was then a manufacturer's rep, but, as we hit balls I noticed that he wasn't much better at this sport than I was. I began to think that if the "Football Player of the First Half-Century" wasn't much better than I am, perhaps I shouldn't put all this effort into trying to hit a golf ball straight.

To put the game of golf in its ultimate framework, one more tournament recap from Tedesco's Len Clark should do the trick. As we said earlier, Len was a delight on the golf course but would not be ranked as highly in terms of golfing ability. In a consolation match in the club's annual "Four-Ball," Len and his partner came to the last hole in their match, which was also the 9th hole, a par 5. The match was all-even and Len had the only shot on the hole.

Unfortunately, he had pulled his third shot badly to the left behind a stand of trees which totally blocked him from the small green. A number of people were in the gallery, including Bill Hoelle who had won the Crosby Pro-Am with professional Art Bell in 1951. He also was the man that had first put the "Chiquita" sticker on the bananas. What they were about to witness holds a rare place in the annals of golf.

Len went to his bag and pulled out what would be the only club that could get the ball over the trees, an open-faced wedge. Hoelle noticed, however, that Len's wedge looked more like a three-iron. Sure enough, Len also noticed the mistake and went back to the bag to get the correct club. Instead, he came back with a three-wood.

Before anyone could voice an alarm, Len had smashed the three-wood into the stand of trees, listening intently as the ball bounced off several limbs and branches. The ball somehow ended up on the green. He two-putted and with his extra stroke on the card, won the hole and the match.

"What were you thinking as you hit your three-wood at the stand of trees?" Len was asked later by another member.

"I knew a three iron was just not enough club," was his simple and direct answer.

The actual truth is whether we like it or not, some of us are destined to be U.S. Open champions, and others are destined to forever play along the far right side of every fairway they will ever walk.

Incurable optimists might say that all things change. Golf, they say, could hit another boom. Except for one thing: We're out of land on most of the old courses that have been popular venues for various major championships, both regional and local. Even the non-championship courses are out of land. My guess is that if we could all come back in a hundred years, a considerable number of our private golf clubs will not exist at all in crowded urban areas.

I would ask that all those in the management of golf, from state associations to club boards re-examine the simplicity of those early days when the game was starting to expand after World War II.

And, here's the question of the day: "Have we, as golfers, allowed the various manufacturers of golf balls and clubs to force changes in the length and difficulty of our current courses or did the players simply get stronger and longer?" I think we now know that we haven't been paying close enough attention to what we've done to ourselves and to our courses. As for business entertainment and particularly the use of corporate jets, while those days are not totally gone, they have been severely curtailed.

I had the opportunity two summers ago to play a course in Westport Harbor, Massachusetts, called Acoaxet. It was the perfect blend of beauty, economics, and golfing enjoyment. My wife and I were invited by a wonderful college classmate, and long-time friend, Bernie Taradash. Bernie was the coxswain on several early 1950s heavyweight crews at the University of Pennsylvania and is now a financial advisor at Oppenheimer & Company in Fall River, Massachusetts. I recorded the name of his company, hoping this would get me invited again.

His course is nine holes, alongside Rhode Island Sound, with breathtaking views, requiring minimum maintenance in key summer months. The clubhouse is an older, classical wooden design with a large porch and an equally large dining room that serves as party room and card room. Concerts and plays can be performed in the room as well. They have a second wooden building for a shower and a change of clothing.

The club started in 1919 and has had normal repairs over time. For the membership, it has served them well without enormous expense. It could be a model for local community golf and in some cases even for certain newly built private courses.

I've saved the most amazing part of the Acoaxet story for last. The club has 800 members and if they wanted more, they could probably get them easily. They come to the area for summer activities, including golf, and the amount of play is such that it does not operate under crowded conditions. They have 350 members signed up for golf and have starting times for mid-summer play.

In the meantime, get in your car and visit a "country course" upstate, or downstate, whichever direction makes sense. Odds are there will be an inexpensive inn or hotel nearby with a great dinner and overnight accommodations. And you are back home before the next noon.

Pick up any golf publication and you'll find beautiful and relatively inexpensive courses all over the place! If you're married, take a compatible couple with you. Or take your kids if they are old enough. Get on an airplane and spend a week playing the courses in southern Spain, or in Portugal. Or, even Italy, now that the country has over 250 courses to choose from. You can learn to yell "fore" in another language. Call a golf travel agent. They can put a trip together that is far less expensive than you thought. There are wonderful barge trips that travel the famous European rivers, stopping each day in a new town for golf and shopping.

The game should be played on a beautiful setting. It should be played for $2 and a beer. Once in a while, don't even bother with a scorecard.

At least once a week it should be played in the late afternoon, as relaxing as any pastime can get.

With a grandchild if possible. And soon.